W9-ASG-814

# Group-Centered Prevention Programs
# for At-Risk Students

Elaine Clanton Harpine

# Group-Centered Prevention Programs for At-Risk Students

 Springer

Elaine Clanton Harpine
University of South Carolina Aiken
471 University Parkway
Aiken, SC 29801
USA
clantonharpine@hotmail.com

ISBN 978-1-4419-7247-7        e-ISBN 978-1-4419-7248-4
DOI 10.1007/978-1-4419-7248-4
Springer New York Dordrecht Heidelberg London

Library of Congress Control Number: 2010938441

© Springer Science+Business Media, LLC 2011
All rights reserved. This work may not be translated or copied in whole or in part without the written permission of the publisher (Springer Science+Business Media, LLC, 233 Spring Street, New York, NY 10013, USA), except for brief excerpts in connection with reviews or scholarly analysis. Use in connection with any form of information storage and retrieval, electronic adaptation, computer software, or by similar or dissimilar methodology now known or hereafter developed is forbidden.
The use in this publication of trade names, trademarks, service marks, and similar terms, even if they are not identified as such, is not to be taken as an expression of opinion as to whether or not they are subject to proprietary rights.

Printed on acid-free paper

Springer is part of Springer Science+Business Media (www.springer.com)

*To my loving husband, Bill, for his
never-ending support and encouragement.*

# Preface

This book is written for those who wish to learn how to use group-centered prevention programs in school-based settings. School-based settings not only include venues during school hours, but also before school, after school, and community-related programs for school children.

Prevention has become a major focus in school-based mental health; many counselors, community organizations, and after school programmers are seeking resources to help fill this need. This book has been written in response to such programming needs and outlines the theoretical structure for developing and implementing group-centered prevention programs. Group-centered prevention programs may be used by psychologists, school counselors, social workers, school-based health practitioners, teachers, parents, and community-based organizations working with children and teens.

A group-centered prevention program combines the learning and psychological needs of students. Group-centered prevention programs develop cognitive, affective, and behavioral skills through structured hands-on group sessions.

Many school counselors have limited training in designing and facilitating group prevention programs with children and teens. This book can serve as a training manual or as supplemental reading. This book can also benefit the group specialist seeking to fine tune skills as well as the beginning practitioner with no group experience. By the end of this book, the reader should have the background, the theory, and the application to use group-centered prevention programs in a school or community setting.

This is the second in a series on school-based mental health. The first book, *Group Interventions in Schools: Promoting Mental Health for At-Risk Children and Youth* (2008), introduced the concept of group-centered interventions in school-based settings. This book takes the next step in the formulation of the group-centered theory, focusing on using group-centered interventions as both an avenue for preventing at-risk behaviors and as a means of correcting or changing dysfunctional behaviors. Additionally, this book introduces a new form of group-centered intervention. While the first book stressed the 1-hour pull-out style intervention, this book focuses on week-long intensive prevention programs.

There are three types of group-centered interventions: (1) 1-hour independent group-centered interventions used in traditional pull-out counseling sessions such as the interventions presented at the end of each chapter, (2) intensive week-long special focus motivational group-centered prevention programs such as the *Camp Sharigan* program, and (3) year-long after school group-centered programs such as *The Reading Orienteering Club,* also discussed in this book.

Motivational group-centered prevention programs such as *Camp Sharigan* and *The Reading Orienteering Club* are discussed throughout the book, but neither program can be contained in their entirety in this book because of their length. *Camp Sharigan* (Clanton Harpine 2010a) is a ready-to-use 10 hour, week-long hands-on program. It comes complete with patterns, learning center booklets, and games. We will discuss the theoretical structure of developing such a week-long special focus intensive motivational group-centered prevention program, but the *Camp Sharigan* program is too lengthy to include in an appendix. It is a complete ready-to-use program packet. *The Reading Orienteering Club* (Clanton Harpine 2011) is a ready-to-use program packet for a year-long weekly program. It encompasses three volumes. For those who are interested in learning more about the *Camp Sharigan* program or *The Reading Orienteering Club* after school program, please feel free to contact me at clantonharpine@hotmail.com

For this book series on group-centered interventions, we have chosen to write small books, approximately 100 pages in length, rather than one long textbook length manuscript because we believe that this will make the books more useable. The first book, *Group Interventions in Schools,* could easily be included as supplemental reading for any undergraduate or graduate class discussing group interventions, schools, school-age children, or issues in educational psychology. In this, the second book in the series, I discuss the development and application of group-centered interventions more in depth, especially as they relate to prevention programming. Such an orientation makes this book an excellent supplement for any psychology or education class wishing to incorporate prevention science and/or group theory. It could also be used by counselors, parenting groups, or teachers wanting to understand the school-based mental health approach. It is also an excellent hands-on guide for developing group-centered prevention programs. I include step-by-step instructions for developing group-centered prevention programs that may be used in a program design class, workshop, in a community organization, or by individual counselors or teachers developing programs at their school. Both books are written in an easy reading style, packed with real-world examples from classrooms, schools, and community-based programs. The brief, 100+ page length, makes these books an excellent choice for workshops, continuing education courses, in-service training, or those who wish to add to their knowledge in group counseling but have limited time for study. Each book is packed with theoretical depth, current references, and ready-to-use exercises which have been tested in real-world settings.

A ready-to-use group-centered intervention is included at the end of each chapter. For some interventions, I give suggestions for expanding beyond the intervention into a week- or month-long program. Several of the ready-to-use group-centered interventions demonstrate how learning centers can be used in group programming. I have chosen to place these interventions at the end of the chapters rather than in a compiled appendix because each group-centered intervention has been selected to represent a specific theoretical concept. Interventions have been placed with the theoretical concept they best illustrate. This is important because the ready-to-use interventions are more than just a quick easy-to-use resource; they are a teaching tool. Their purpose is to illustrate how each theoretical principle can be implemented and used in a real program. To make it easier for those using the book and wishing to search for a particular intervention, I have included a special table of contents listing all of the interventions and highlighting some of the ways they might be used. This easy reference will make it easier to select an intervention at a glance.

Each chapter begins with a brief case study example from a group-centered prevention program, and ends with a programming design exercise and a ready-to-use group-centered intervention that reinforces the chapter's theoretical principles and demonstrates the programming design techniques being taught. Both of the books in this series may be used in conjunction with each other or independently.

Chapter 1 introduces the two program examples used throughout the text. Chapter 2 explains why our present approach to group programming is not working in the schools and introduces step-by-step instructions for developing an effective group program. Chapter 3 discusses how to organize a group, incorporating basic group theory and also the needs of counselors today. Chapter 4 emphasizes the importance of analyzing your group and evaluating the needs of group members in depth before introducing a new program. Chapter 5 illustrates how to use the power of group process to bring about change. Chapter 6 stresses the advantages of intrinsic motivation in group programs. Chapter 7 describes how to create interactive situations in group programs and the importance interaction plays in group theory. Chapter 8 outlines how to build an instructional learning component into a group program. Chapter 9 adds the therapeutic factor. Chapter 10 focuses on transferring what has been learned back to the classroom.

## Easy Reference Guide to Group-Centered Interventions

**Age level**: Kindergarten through 2nd Grade
**Learning Objective:** To increase word recognition skills for the letter A through hands-on activities.
**Counseling Objective:** To rebuild self-efficacy by teaching the beginning word decoding skills necessary to learn to read.
**Time needed:** 2 hours. This activity can be expanded and used across a six-month study of the vowel sounds. You simply make a new balloon and add the new vowel sound.

**Age level:** High School
**Learning Objective:** To enhance writing skills through a reflective, critical thinking group activity.

**Counseling Objective:** To enhance the development of individual responsibility and to strengthen problem solving group skills.

**Time needed:** 1 or 2 hours (depending on whether the story is read as a group or as a homework assignment). This group-centered intervention can easily be expanded into a week-long or month-long research writing project.

**Age level:** 2nd Grade through High School

**Learning Objective:** To initiate self awareness and group interaction and help group members identify feelings and experiences that they have in common.

**Counseling Objective:** To initiate interaction and to build group cohesion.

**Time needed:** 2 hours, depending on the size of the group. You may also use the name tags for several early sessions in the group to help initiate interaction.

**Age level:** Any age

**Learning Objective:** To enhance student's ability to distinguish vowel sounds and match vowel sounds through a hands-on activity.

**Counseling Objective:** To strengthen group skills and enhance the curative power of group process.

**Time needed:** 1 hour-can be repeated with new words. This intervention can be repeated with new words and developed into a week-long or month-long activity using different words and sentences.

**Age level:** Any age

**Learning Objective:** To motivate students to write grammatically correct stories.

**Counseling Objective:** To generate intrinsic motivation through a hands-on project.

**Time needed:** 1 hour. A simple pop-up house book may be expanded into a writing project that might encompass a week or month-long project. All you need to add is the writing assignment.

**Age level:** Older elementary and middle school

**Learning Objective:** To increase reading and writing skills and polish proper etiquette through hands-on activities.

**Counseling Objective:** To increase interaction and the development of the group.

**Time needed:** Divided into three 1-hour sessions. Your school or community group may decide to host a special *Manners Please* week or month in which groups or classes practice etiquette.

**Age level:** Third Grade through Eighth Grade

**Learning Objective:** To increase comprehension when reading through hands-on activities.

**Counseling Objective:** To enhance acceptance of others in a group.

**Time needed:** 1–2 weeks, depending how many pages of the story you wish to do a day. You can use the story for a one day activity, across a two week period, completing three pages a day, or expand the project into a month-long activity.

**Age level:** This is an excellent intervention for older elementary, middle school, and high school students.

**Learning Objective:** To develop and strengthen vocabulary skills and phonological skills.

**Counseling Objective:** To enhance group cohesion and to teach group skills through teamwork.

**Time needed:** 1 week or 5 hours: This group-centered intervention works well with older students who need to work on phonics. You can have students simply read the puppet play or you can expand this intervention by allowing the students to present the puppet play to possibly a younger group of children.

University of South Carolina Aiken                            Elaine Clanton Harpine
471 University Parkway
Aiken, SC 29801
USA
clantonharpine@hotmail.com

# Acknowledgments

I wish to express my appreciation to Judy Jones, my editor and friend, for her support and help in the development of this book series on group-centered interventions. I would also like to thank my husband for his love and support throughout the entire project and for his patience and helpful comments on the text, as well as my three children, David, Virginia, and Christina, who have all worked as reading tutors in my *Camp Sharigan* program over the years. A thank you also goes to all of the children, youth, university students, community volunteers, parents, teachers, and university faculty who I have had the pleasure of working with while developing group-centered prevention programs.

# Contents

# About the Author

Elaine Clanton Harpine, Ph.D., is a motivational psychologist specializing in group-centered motivational program design. She has 38 years experience designing and conducting motivational programs for children and youth. Dr. Clanton Harpine earned her doctorate in Educational Psychology, Counseling from the University of Illinois, Urbana-Champaign.

Dr. Clanton Harpine has published 10 nonfiction books, including *Group Interventions in Schools: Promoting Mental Health for At-Risk Children and Youth* (2008), and *No Experience Necessary!* which received an *Award of Excellence* in 1995 and was selected as one of the top five children's books in its class. Other published children's writings include a two volume series entitled, *Come Follow Me*, in 2001, a three-volume family series completed in 2003, a youth book in 1989, along with numerous articles for teenagers on peer pressure, coping with failure, alcohol abuse, parents, suicide, and more recently, articles on using group-centered interventions in the schools. Other published writings include a series on *Erasing Failure in the Classroom,* a series of ready-to-use group-centered program packets: Vol. 1, the *Camp Sharigan* program (*2nd ed.*, 2010) and Vol. 2, *Vowel Clustering* (2010). The program packet for the *Reading Orienteering Club* (Vol. 3.) is scheduled for release in 2011.

Dr. Clanton Harpine has been interviewed on local early morning television and radio regarding her workshop "Communication for Married Couples" and has been interviewed on local university radio regarding her work with inner city children.

Her research for the past 9 years has focused on using group-centered interventions with at-risk readers. Dr. Clanton Harpine designed the motivational reading program called *Camp Sharigan,* which she has used extensively in her work and research. She also designed *The Reading Orienteering Club* after school program and *4-Step Method* for teaching at-risk children to read. Her research with these programs has been published in psychological journals and reported through presentations at the American Psychological Association's annual conventions.

In recent years, Dr. Clanton Harpine has been teaching Group Therapy and Counseling, Lifespan Development, and Human Growth and Development at the

University of South Carolina Aiken and is continuing her research with group-centered interventions. She is the editor for the "Prevention Corner" column which appears quarterly in *The Group Psychologist*. She was selected for inclusion in *Who's Who of American Women*, 2006–2010, for her work with children in inner city neighborhoods.

# Chapter 1
# Introduction

*He was in third grade, reading at the preprimer level (below first grade). His mother said, "he hates to read." On the second day of Camp Sharigan, he begged his mother, "Just a few more minutes, please, I want to finish the story."*

After school and community-based prevention programs offer an excellent opportunity for at-risk children (McWhirter et al. 2007) to learn concepts through hands-on interventions that they were unable to learn in a regular classroom. This book focuses on developing week-long group-centered prevention programs and gives step-by-step directions for developing such programs. The emphasis is on how to combine the learning and counseling needs into one single program through the *school-based mental health approach*. Week-long intensive programs are becoming more popular in school-based settings as research highlights their impact. Even though the examples that I use throughout the book highlight reading and the *Camp Sharigan Project*, the same procedure can be used to design any school-based group-centered prevention program.

The *Camp Sharigan* program is a portable group-centered prevention program which utilizes the *school-based mental health approach* by stressing both the academic and psychological needs of students. *Camp Sharigan* is a week-long hands-on program which uses a summer camp setting. The camp features a make-believe paper *poison ivy vine, tricky words, Mount Reading, Lake Read*, daily *treasure hunt maps*, and the *Road to Nowhere but Reading*. The program is contained in a complete ready-to-use packet (Clanton Harpine 2010a) which can be used by anyone in any kind of setting.

I travel around the country directing the *Camp Sharigan* project. I have worked with children and teens who were expelled from the public school system in Tampa, children from the projects in Chicago, private and public school children in the Bronx, children from inner city neighborhood schools in Ohio classified as failing schools, the lowest scoring at-risk readers in a suburban midwestern school, at-risk children and teens in both South Carolina and Georgia, states with two of the highest high school dropout rates in the nation, and Hispanic immigrant, English as a second language children in Texas. I mostly work with after school programs, either through schools or community-based organizations.

Clanton Harpine, *Group-Centered Prevention Programs for At-Risk Students*, DOI 10.1007/978-1-4419-7248-4_1, © Springer Science+Business Media, LLC 2011

I typically travel with a team, either middle school, high school, or college age, but sometimes I train workers on site, as was the case at one particular location where I trained sixth grade students to work as reading tutors for a program with first through third graders. The community center assigned me to use the computer lab for *Camp Sharigan*. The room looked entirely too small for 30 first through third graders, 10 sixth grade helpers, and all of the hands-on props which accompany *Camp Sharigan*. Computers and tables lined the walls; so I hung the cloth wall hangings high so that they would drape over the computers. All chairs were removed. The ten learning centers were arranged on the floor around the room. Each learning center had a program packet notebook in which step-by-step instructions for that learning center were contained for the entire 10-hour program. I held a 2-hours training session for the sixth grade helpers. All the sixth grade helpers needed to do was help the children read and follow the directions at each learning center station. The learning centers provided both the skill building and group counseling interventions used in the program. The week was a great success (Clanton Harpine and Reid 2009a). *Camp Sharigan* functioned well in a tiny room with only sixth grade helpers because I used a program packet instead of a training manual. One of this book's goals is to demonstrate how to develop a program packet for a group-centered prevention program.

When I am working near home, university students serve as the hands-on tutors. *Camp Sharigan* provides an excellent hands-on learning laboratory in which university students can learn how to work with at-risk children and teens. Service-learning, internships, or any hands-on learning endeavor turns the university classroom into a learning laboratory. The *school-based mental health approach* provides hands-on programs where university students can test out theories from the text and learn to apply textbook theories to real world situations (Clanton Harpine 2007b).

The programs I design can be used during the normal school day. For example, a school might decide to use the *Camp Sharigan* program for a special week-long emphasis on reading. Fourth and fifth graders could work as reading tutors and assist first through third graders through the program. The library, gymnasium, or even a cluster of classrooms can be used for the camp. Students can be rotated through the program at different intervals so that every student may benefit. Unfortunately, most schools are too frantic over mandated testing to consider anything other than a barrage of test prep booklets and practice tests; therefore, I work primarily with after school prevention programs. The *school-based mental health approach* provides the structure for developing programs which meet both the educational and counseling needs of students.

## *Step 1: Type of Program*

What type of prevention program do you plan to design–1 week, 6 weeks, 1 year?

# Chapter 2
# Creating At-Risk Children and Youth

*She entered the room wearing a slightly soiled bulky winter coat with fake fur trim around the hood. The hood completely covered her face. She was much taller than I was and did not seem to be the least bit excited about my idea to organize a new group. As one of my University students told me later, "I thought she was going to hit you." I, too, was not entirely certain that she was not planning violence. Her body posture was definitely aggressive. Ignoring her obvious signs of hostility, I suggested that we all find a chair. Three teens, middle school and high school age, two of my university students, and myself were stuffed in an overly crowded computer lab at a local community center. I explained that the six of us would be meeting each week. Sometimes we would meet as a group, sometimes for one-on-one tutoring, but that every Thursday we would come to this room to work on reading. She sat defiant with her hood still pulled over her head hiding her face. We broke into one-on-one subgroups for testing and initial tutoring. She was 15 years of age, a freshman in high school, and reading at the pre-primer (below first grade) level. The school had placed her in a special education classroom and had designated that she was to be taught second grade course material. She had an extensive record of behavioral issues and had been removed from the school bus because of bad behavior. Her file was marked "will most likely drop out of school as soon as she is old enough." There was absolutely no way she could read the second grade material being given to her at school.*

*Six months later she was greeting me with a smile and a hug, reading first-grade material, and asking if I thought she'd be able to go to college, possibly a 2-year school, when she graduated from high school.*

Four million children and teens between the ages of 9 and 17 years can be classified as suffering from a major mental illness and approximately 21% of school-age children and teens have a diagnosable mental illness or addictive disorder and are thereby labeled as being at-risk (US Public Health Service 2000). When counselors or psychologists use the term "at-risk," they typically are referring to someone who is suffering from an emotional or adjustment problem (McWhirter et al. 2007). When teachers and the schools use the term "at-risk," they are probably referring to students who are at risk of dropping out of school or at risk of failure, but academic failure always comes with adjustment problems (Flaherty and Osher 2003; Weist 1997). Academic failure and psychological adjustment go hand-in-hand, and academic failure in the classroom can place any student in the psychological at-risk category, regardless of whether they come from an affluent neighborhood with well-funded schools or a poor neighborhood. For children who have been labeled at-risk, *the school-based mental health approach* can mean the difference between success and failure.

Academic failure is closely tied to psychological development because failure is a form of rejection. The classroom becomes one of the first social arenas beyond the family in which the child seeks membership. Learning in school takes place in front of peers. Being labeled as a failure in the classroom can be especially damaging to young students (Rudolph et al. 2001) because failure to obtain a classroom goal, such as reading, becomes a roadblock to acceptance. Peer group rejection becomes intertwined with the child's perception of themselves. Children often feel shunned, ostracized, or labeled. If classroom failure continues, then the child will internalize such failure as part of their self-concept. Students fear being different than other students; they fear not being able to fit in with the group. The inability to succeed in the classroom is perceived as the inability to acquire the skills necessary to join the classroom group – to be as good as others in the group.

## The Role of Prevention

A growing body of evidence shows that prevention programs can improve a child's ability to learn and overall psychological wellness (Nelson et al. 2003). Therefore, the goal of the *school-based mental health approach* is to create group prevention programs which strengthen school-based mental health through rebuilding necessary skills. The group becomes an early prevention tool for improving psychological adjustment and mental well-being. The *school-based mental health approach* provides a step-by-step model for designing and developing group prevention programs in schools and community settings. The *school-based mental health approach* combines counseling and learning and makes full use of interaction and group process, stresses intrinsic (internal) motivation rather than extrinsic (rewards or prizes), and focuses on self-efficacy (belief that the student can accomplish a task) rather than self-esteem (feeling good about oneself). Group-centered prevention programs organized before school, during school, and after school can help today's children have a more successful life, today and tomorrow.

To undo the psychological damage caused by school failure, it is necessary to prevent and erase classroom failure (Brooks-Gunn 2003). Before we can organize groups to prevent academic and psychological failure, however, we need to understand what causes children to be labeled at-risk and in need of counseling.

## How Families Help Create At-Risk Children and Youth

Unfortunately many children are at risk before they are even born. Risk begins at the moment of conception. The fertilized ovum carries the effects of the parents' life style within its DNA and cells, not only the inherited traits. Four weeks after conception, the brain, heart, ears, eyes, nose, mouth, arms, and legs are beginning to form. Many women are not even fully aware that they are pregnant by the fourth week after conception, yet the brain is already developing and the head and brain will soon comprise 50% of the embryo's total size. The nervous system and brain waves are functioning by the fifth week, and as many as 100,000 neurons are produced every minute (Nelson and Bosquet 2000).

*Risk factors during pregnancy.* The brain will continue to develop throughout the fetal stage and be influenced by everything the mother consumes. Aspirin, ibuprofen, and even birth control pills taken by a woman before she realizes that she's pregnant affect the developing brain of the unborn child. Illicit drugs carry an even heavier risk. "Crack" cocaine use during pregnancy has been linked with lower IQ scores (Richardson et al. 2008), problems with language development, comprehension, verbal expression, and auditory attention (Lewis et al. 2004). Alcohol, nicotine, and caffeine all also affect brain development. As little as one ounce of alcohol can damage the brain of the unborn child and cause verbal learning deficits, attention difficulties, and below average mental development (Cornelius et al. 2002). Nicotine reduces the oxygen content of the mother's blood, thereby reducing the amount of oxygen available to the unborn child and the developing brain. Secondhand smoke may be even more damaging. Children whose mothers smoke marijuana during pregnancy often struggle more in spelling, reading, particularly reading comprehension, and may suffer from anxiety and depression (Goldschmidt et al. 2004). Smoking, alcohol, and drug use during pregnancy cause many other birth defects and physically debilitating problems (fetal alcohol syndrome, cleft palate, tremors, sleep disorders, and other emotional problems), but the focus here will be on academic at-risk problems. I call it simply SAD, because Smoking, Alcohol, and Drugs sentence many children to a lifetime of at-risk behaviors and problems before the child is even born, and some of these conditions can never be erased. This is true of children born to wealthy parents in affluent neighborhoods as well as children born in poverty.

*Family risk factors after the child is born.* A newborn is born with 100–200 billion basic brain cells or neurons, but these neurons have very few connections. In an adult, one neuron may have over 5,000 connections. These neuron connections are essential for the child to learn. Changes in the connections between neurons enable the child to learn and establishes a foundation for cognitive development (Merzenich 2001).

During the first 2 years of life the baby's brain is rapidly growing and developing. From birth to 1 year, the child begins to learn the language spoken by those with whom the child lives. By age 3 years, the child begins to assimilate the grammatical sentence structure of the language. If the parent reads books to the young child during the first few years of life, grammatical sentence structure is enhanced, but even if the child does not have the benefit of listening to stories or books, the child will learn to speak. Learning to speak is a natural process. All children, unless confronted with physical inability, learn to speak. This is not true of reading. Reading, spelling, and written grammatical sentence structure must be taught.

## How Schools Help Create At-Risk Children and Youth

The guiding principle of any educational system should be: What is truly best for the students, both academically and psychologically? Cost, administrative concerns, mandated testing, classroom management, or the well-intended advice of others must not become the directing principles upon which programs are developed. If we are to create successful mental health programs, the primary concern must be based on the needs of the students. This is not always true in the public school system.

For instance, the U.S. Department of Education's *Blue Ribbon Schools Program*, part of the *No Child Left Behind* initiative vividly demonstrates an important lesson. Statistical standards, not student needs, are used to measure excellence in schools. The following is one example.

A blue ribbon school, considered to be the best school in its district, teaches through the use of video instruction and worksheets. Teachers are forbidden to introduce new ideas, or even to work out a math problem on the chalkboard; all instruction comes from the video. The administration maintains an iron grip on what is and is not taught each day. Everything is geared to mandated testing, state benchmark standards, and increasing test scores. There is no time for individualized instruction. If a student fails a test, the student forfeits recess to retake the test. The school does not re-teach the material, only retests and continues retesting. There is one method of instruction and only one method; children are taught through videos and a barrage of worksheets. Testing begins as the children enter the door each day and concludes with a daily minimum of 12 worksheets, quizzes, or tests before they leave their desks to go home. It is literally one worksheet after another. A child who falls behind is lost. Such "robotic-style teaching," as the teachers themselves refer to the approach with which they are required to teach, creates at-risk students and psychological adjustment problems.

Does this blue ribbon school meet the needs of its students? No, the needs of students are buried beneath mountains of worksheets and test data. The blue ribbon school does not have time to be concerned with the individual learning needs or psychological needs of students because the blue ribbon school must maintain test scores at all costs, even at the cost of the mental health needs of the students. This type of teaching approach has led many researchers to call for system-wide change (Greenberg et al. 2003; Weissberg et al. 2003). A year-long stream of stressful standardized tests or worksheets does not contribute to mental health and well-being (Sternberg et al. 1997). Standardized tests measure only a small fraction of the skills and expertise needed to be successful in life (Sternberg and Grigorenko 2002). Mandated testing and a never-ending sea of workbook pages are also not consistent with current educational research (Kaplan et al. 2009). While many call for change in our communities and in our schools, today's children cannot wait for tomorrow's changes. Children sitting in class today, need help today.

The *school-based mental health approach* combines academic and psychological needs through group-centered prevention programs which work directly with at-risk students; therefore, our focus in this book will be on developing intensive group-centered prevention programs which can be used in school-based and community settings to foster psychological development and well-being as well as academic success.

## How School Counselors and Psychologists Help Create At-Risk Children and Youth

Schools are the primary source for mental health services for children (Brown and Tracy 2008), and children only get one chance to be successful in the public school system (Weinstein 2006). Mandated testing and the all-encompassing quest for test scores have reduced mental health services in schools (Maras et al. 2008). There is also an ever-widening gap between research and practice in school-based mental health (Wandersman et al. 2008; Weist and Paternite 2006). Many complain that evidence-based results are not transferring to the real-world setting of the classroom which has led to a call for change in how we deliver mental health services in schools (Adelman and Taylor 2006; Wandersman and Florin 2003; Weisz et al. 2004).

Many school counselors believe that their counseling efforts have been compromised by budget cuts, extra job assignments, and mandated testing. As one counselor explained, "When am I supposed to pull students out for counseling sessions? I have bus duty before school, cafeteria duty and recess during lunch, bus duty after school, and in between I'm in charge of locker assignments and schedule changes. I gave six students a detention during lunch; it's a safe bet those six are not coming to my office in search of counseling." When counselors become disciplinarians or on-duty officers, they lose the opportunity to get to know students in a nonthreatening situation. Students rarely turn for help or disclose problems and fears to those who administer discipline. Such mandatory assignments in school settings destroy the counselor-client relationship.

Other counselors complain that teachers are so pressured by mandated testing that they will no longer allow students to attend counseling sessions during class time. Parents are reluctant to sign their children up for counseling because they, too, do not want to see children miss classroom material which might be covered on end-of-the-year tests. School counselors have been reduced to giving short talks to classes, sorting out class schedules, and meeting with students only after they have been identified as major discipline problems. Preventive counseling is almost nonexistent in today's schools. As Martin Seligman points out in his book, *The Optimistic Child* (2007), counselors need to spend as much time, if not more, on prevention rather than waiting until treatment is critical.

Counseling in public school settings must change. Our approach to counseling in schools is not working. Yet, over 70% of children's counseling groups take place in the school (Hoag and Burlingame 1997). A new approach is needed. The *school-based mental health approach* offers a new method for working with at-risk students which addresses the academic needs and the psychological needs of the student who has been labeled at-risk.

*Schools blame children when they fail to learn.* In the example of the 15-year-old high school freshman at the beginning of the chapter, the young teen had learned most of her consonant sounds but virtually none of her vowel sounds, not even the long vowel sounds. The school's approach to teaching her to read was to give her short word lists to memorize, such as the days of the week on flash cards. The school's rationale for using second grade reading instructional material, when the student could not even read at the pre-primer level (below first grade), was that they wanted to challenge the student. Over and over the 15-year-old had been told that she was "lazy" and "not trying," or that "she is a slow learner but could read if she would just apply herself to the task." Unfortunately, she could not read because she bore the residual effects of her mother using "crack" cocaine during pregnancy and the fact that the school which she attended was still hanging on to a whole language approach to reading. Whole language has created more at-risk readers than probably any other method ever developed (Foorman et al. 2003). As soon as I started teaching *vowel clustering* (Clanton Harpine 2010b), a method for teaching phonics to at-risk readers, the young teen began to read. Progress has been slow, but she is reading, and she is so very excited to be able to do so. She has even agreed to work with me over the summer. During the fall, we selected a first-grade level book as our goal. She said, "that's a book I've always wanted to read." She hopes to be able to read the book to her little brother by Christmas. As her self-efficacy improved (belief that she could learn to read), and she saw herself actually reading, the anger, the aggression, and the threat of violence melted away. Even her behavior at school improved. Learning to read has truly changed her life, her psychological well-being, and her prospects for the future, which is what we strive for in counseling. When we addressed the root cause of her behavior problem, her behavior was no longer a problem. She is still terrified that one of the members of her peer group will find out that she cannot read, or that she's reading "baby" books, as she calls the early reading material we are working with, but her joy and excitement from being able to read are so strong that she comes back week after week just so that she can learn to read.

*Reading failure fuels mental health problems.* As many as one fourth of all public school students suffer from some form of psychological adjustment problem (Satcher 2000); many of these adjustment problems stem from academic failure. Weak reading skills contribute to many mental health problems that counselors, teachers, and parents encounter among school children. Learning to read is essential to healthy early child development. In 2009, approximately 40% of fourth-grade children were unable to read at grade level (National Assessment of Educational Progress 2009). Seventy-five percent of children who do not learn to read by the end of third grade never learn to read at grade level (Lyon 2002; Lyon 1998). Reading failure leads to frustration, anger, aggression, bullying, and even violence (Bryant et al. 2003).

Reading failure is at the center of most mental health at-risk problems found in the schools. Reading failure can lead to aggressive school violence (Catalano et al. 2003), dropping out of school before graduation (Nastasi et al. 2004), adolescent substance abuse (Sussman et al. 2004), negative self-evaluations (Berking et al. 2008), anxiety, and even depression (Herman et al. 2008). Interventions which reduce reading failure have been shown to also reduce the risk of depression and other psychological at-risk behaviors (Fleming et al. 2004; Keller and Just 2009). Erasing reading failure should therefore become one of our earliest school-based mental health preventive concerns because reading failure causes lifelong psychological damage (Criss et al. 2002).

## How Communities Help Create At-Risk Children and Youth

The community's involvement in school-based mental health has been steadily growing over the past 10 years. After-school programs, sometimes at the school, sometimes at community centers, are becoming more prevalent. After-school community programs have the potential to provide mental health services in a troubled community. Community programs can fill the gap between school and home with something more than just child care. Community programs can serve as vital school-based mental health prevention centers.

All too often, though, in school-based mental health, we design programs in schools and in the community to fit the needs of the adults who are conducting the program rather than the needs of the students who are participating in the program. An example from a community-based after-school group highlights the danger of such an approach. When the group met to decide how to organize their program, they did not consider what would work best with at-risk children; instead, they proposed formats that echoed their own personal beliefs. (1) A former school teacher wanted to have the children sitting in rows silently working on worksheets; (2) another teacher wanted direct instruction by a qualified teacher and homework assignments; (3) a retired businessman suggested just sitting and listening to the children read; and (4) another well-intended worker said, "All of this stuff is just a waste of time; children need to sit down and do as they are told." The group finally sought the advice of someone who worked with at-risk children and organized their program along the guidelines given by their at-risk advisor. The group then spent the entire 2 months of their program's existence trying to reshape and undo everything the outside advisor had taught them. They spent every day trying to restore their original concept: sitting in rows doing homework pages. The needs of the children were never discussed during the actual implementation of the program. The program format chosen and the at-risk expert were wasted because the directors were unwilling to deviate from their personal beliefs. The focus was on them, not the needs of the children.

Another example of good intentions that did not work comes from an after-school program for children and teens from a drug-infested neighborhood. The group was based at a local church; the volunteers worked hard and were sincere, and their enthusiasm within the group was contagious. Research indicates that religiosity works as a deterrent to alcohol and substance abuse as well as risky sexual behavior with teens (Wills et al. 2003), and more and more churches are developing prevention programs.

At one session, a short middle-aged woman dressed in blue jeans and a T-shirt shouted, "Get back, Satan!" As she spoke to the group of 45 children and youth ranging from kindergarten age to high school age, she demanded that the children and teens resist temptation and walk away from drugs and alcohol. Religious zeal and fear comprised her prevention technique. She even invited volunteers to come forward and demonstrate how to turn away from the temptation of drugs. Her demonstration consisted of teaching the youth to point and repeat the phrase: "Get back, Satan! I'm not following you." The session was lively; no one dozed off. Her desire to prevent drug use was unquestionable, but was her group prevention approach effective? No, adolescents stayed in the program, enjoying the free dinner and activities offered each afternoon and evening until they were old enough to drop out; at that point, street life prevailed. Drugs took over their lives, most dropped out of school, and virtually no one from the group went on to college or to find full-time employment.

Does that mean that community organizations such as churches should not be used for after school prevention programs? Absolutely not, I personally work hand-in-hand with many community church-sponsored groups in providing after-school programs for at-risk children and youth. Churches can provide a wonderful family support structure and an ongoing preventive atmosphere. Spirituality adds an additional deterring effect to prevention programs, but spirituality alone is not enough (Wills et al. 2003) to bring about mental health change and well-being.

## How Evidence-Based Programs Help Create At-Risk Children and Youth

Most schools currently require or strongly suggest using evidence-based programs. If such evidence-based programs are not being used as designed, however, then the research evidence which supports the evidence-based program is worthless to the school that is using it (McHugh and Barlow 2010).

As one well-intended program director told me, "I really like your new program; we're going to use bits and pieces of it." We cannot continue to take programs apart, use bits and pieces, and expect positive results. Evidence-based programs only produce the evidence-based results if they are implemented as designed and used in the research setting (McHugh et al. 2009). If an evidence-based program is redesigned to fit their philosophy of what a program should be, then they are no longer running an evidenced-based program. The person is running bits and pieces of an evidence-based program, and the results will not be the same.

Programs often become distorted when implemented by well-intended but confused school personnel or community group leaders. Let's use a very popular school concept which vividly demonstrates this principle: the open classroom concept.

*The evidence-based program.* The open classroom concept originated in the 1960s and was originally put forth as a theory of curriculum development.

The open classroom concept built upon Dewey's theories of learning-by-doing and working in small cooperative groups (Dewey 1997) as well as the concept of interdisciplinary learning and engaging the whole child in the task of learning (Taba 1962). The original open classroom concept never discussed physically taking down walls or doors or building schools without walls. The original concept was for curriculum development, suggesting hands-on learning techniques, and working with curriculum that engaged children in cooperative small groups, particularly learning centers within the classroom where children could go together, work, and solve a problem and engage in critical thinking. In short, the original open classroom concept wanted teachers to get rid of worksheets and allow children to move around the room working in small groups at learning centers – hence, a "classroom without walls."

*Distorting an evidence-based program through implementation.* Yet, in the 1970s, the open classroom concept was distorted into a massive building campaign which saw school districts building schools without walls, without doors, and in some instances without classrooms. The results were disastrous, which led many to state that the open classroom concept was a failure. Actually, it was the well-intended but distorted implementation of the open classroom concept that had failed (Stenhouse 1975). The most ironic result of building classrooms without walls is that students who still attend class in "buildings without walls" from the 1970s spend more hours in quiet seat work working on worksheets than they do in traditional schools. Extensive seat work is deemed necessary in order to control noise levels.

*Buying an evidence-based program does not guarantee evidence-based implementation.* Schools, after-school programs, and other school-based community organizations working with children and teens genuinely want to provide effective programs, but if the programs offered do not actually end up helping students, then such good intentions are wasted (Kazak et al. 2010). Therefore, simply buying an evidence-based program does not ensure evidence-based implementation or evidence-based results. So, when we organize and plan for a new group, it is not enough to merely have good intentions or say that we are using an evidence-based program. Effective programs must be designed which incorporate the evidence-based design, not just on paper or in a manual, but in the actual implementation of the program. We need a way to guarantee that evidence-based programs are being used as designed and tested.

As long as implementers are free to decide how they should implement, adapt, or change an evidence-based program, evidence-based programs are worthless. Often when groups select bits and pieces of an evidence-based program to add to their own approach, schools or community groups blame the evidence-based program rather than their implementation of the program when research promised results are not forthcoming. There is no way to ensure that a school or community organization will actually use an evidence-based program as it was written and designed to be implemented (Kratochwill 2007). We cannot assume that good intentions will guarantee an effective program, because they do not.

# How Reliance on Manualized Programs Helps Create At-Risk Children and Youth

Many researchers call for more reliance on manuals, but a manual does not guarantee that a program will be implemented using the evidence-based design, because manuals do not guarantee evidence-based practices. This is exemplified by a school which uses the STEMS Word Study Program (Thompson 2000). The STEMS manual discusses teaching "word attack" skills for prefixes, suffixes, and word roots. The manual also emphasizes spelling instruction focused on "word chucks" and looking at how words are related in order to enhance long-term memory. Yet, the school using the program merely distributes a list of STEMS every week for the students to memorize for a test on Friday. The school does not include the instruction, just a list of STEMS on Monday, and a test on Friday. Also, the school does not emphasize spelling. One teacher complained, "I was criticized for trying to correct a student's spelling of the word *government*. The school classified this student as being an 'A' student; yet the student had written 'gov4ment.' I was told that spelling could only be corrected during spelling lessons; for other class work, spelling doesn't matter." The STEMS program and manual was attempting to teach an approach in which spelling could be integrated into every subject and become part of the student's way of thinking. The school's implementation of the program was the use of memorization to raise test scores, but then for anything other than mandated testing, spelling really didn't matter. The school could advertise to parents that they were using an evidence-based program which would result in higher SAT scores, but the school's incorrect use of the program actually rendered the program ineffective, specifically because the school did not use the program as described in the manual.

# Good Intentions Are Not Enough

Manuals, evidence-based programs, research, and good intentions do not help if personnel conducting the program ignore the manual and the research. Therefore, good intentions are not always effective.

How should counselors, psychologists, teachers, parents, community workers, and others approach these school-based mental health problems? Can we as mental health professionals, teachers, parents, and community workers enact changes which will help students? I believe that we can.

In school-based mental health, we need (1) to remind all well-intentioned adults that the needs of students must come first; (2) to ensure that evidence-based programs are used in school and community-based prevention and treatment; and (3) to make sure that evidence-based programs are used correctly, not simply in bits and pieces. Ready-to-use program packets could be one solution which might solve this problem in school-based settings. One of our goals throughout this book will be to discuss designing and implementing group-centered prevention programs using program packets.

# Developing Group-Centered Program Packets

A group-centered program packet is a ready-to-use program which has an educational as well as a counseling or mental health component (Clanton Harpine 2006). The programs are usually interactive and often use hands-on learning techniques. Group-centered program packets are complete and ready to use.

Some program packets, such as the *Reading Orienteering Club* (Clanton Harpine 2011), are year-long programs designed to be used in a public school classroom or community center after school with virtually no prior setup. All the group leader must do is provide paper, pencils, and other basic supplies. The program is divided into ongoing sessions which may be used once a week, twice a week, or even four times a week. The program is presented through hands-on learning center workstations where children work together in small groups or individually. The program is designed to be flexible to the needs of the school or community group without changing the program. Flexibility is built into the program packet.

Another example of a group-centered program packet is the *Camp Sharigan* program (Clanton Harpine 2010a). *Camp Sharigan* is a 10-hour, week-long motivational group-centered prevention program for children in first through third grades. The *Camp Sharigan* program packet utilizes 10 hands-on learning centers set in the atmosphere of a portable summer camp scene. Instructions are given for creating a make-believe portable camp with trees, waterfalls, and even a rainbow which can be taken from school to school to motivate and encourage children to erase reading failure.

The *Camp Sharigan* and *Reading Orienteering Club* packets incorporate hands-on remedial reading teaching techniques and group counseling motivational techniques; therefore, they combine both the educational needs and the counseling needs of at-risk children (Clanton Harpine 2007c). The program packet is a ready-to-use set of hands-on booklets which provide step-by-step learning center instructions – not a manual, but the actual program. The teacher or counselor at the school need only to open the packet and lay out the booklets when they're ready to utilize the program. The packet includes game cards, stories, and puppet plays, as well as all learning center instructional materials (including the step-by-step learning center instructions for the children).

Using a ready-to-use program packet ensures that the hands-on, at-risk teaching methods and the motivational group counseling techniques are used correctly because both techniques are written into the learning center workstation booklets. Therefore, evidence-based programs can be used as intended and the local schools can receive the same evidence-based results as the researcher who developed the program.

Both of these program packets stress erasing reading failure as a means of preventing depressive symptoms, at-risk behaviors, and other mental health concerns. Research shows that improving reading skills does in fact improve mental health and wellness (Maugban et al. 2003). Groups are one of the best preventive techniques in mental health because groups enable children and teens to experience change in a group setting which translates back to the classroom better than one-on-one tutoring (Cleary and Zimmerman 2004).

## Benefits of School Mental Health

Program packets reduce preparation time for school personnel conducting the programs. Program packets will enable psychologists to develop evidence-based programs and ensure that the program will be used as intended, thereby allowing evidence-based results from research to benefit a larger number of children and teens at the local school level. Learning centers allow for individualized, self-paced learning so that the needs of all students can be met. Program packets are one method for bridging the gap between research and practice.

Because an evidence-based program packet may not be available for the particular group you are organizing, it may fall upon you to develop your own program packet. This book provides a step-by-step outline for developing group-centered program packets. Throughout each chapter, you will be given a question-response set of worksheets. Starting with Step 2 in this chapter, work through the series of worksheets and follow the steps to organizing an effective group-centered prevention program.

One of the first steps in designing a group-centered program packet is to analyze the group. When we organize a group, we typically organize a group in response to a particular problem. Note the difference between *what* not *who* is the cause of the problem. All too often we identify students as the problem instead of *what* caused students to have a problem.

## *Step 2: Identify the Problem*

What problem would you like to work on or change?

What (not who) is the primary cause of the problem?

Why is there a need for a change? How will a change benefit the group?

*Each worksheet will be accompanied by a design example.* For each design step presented throughout the book, an example is presented after the worksheet. Examples will help you understand how to use the design worksheet pages and give suggestions for designing your own program. The design examples come from the *Camp Sharigan* week-long motivational group-centered prevention program, but the principles can be applied in any number of different ways.

**Step 2, Design Example**

Because *Camp Sharigan* is our example, our problem is reading failure or inability to read at grade level. The cause of the problem lies with the methods being used in the classroom to teach reading—notice we did not say the problem is the student or the teacher. The cause of the problem is (1) classroom approach does not allow for individuality and the individual learning needs of at-risk students; (2) reading instruction often is taught too early, many kindergarteners are expected to memorize 50 or 60 words and/or begin reading; (3) only one method is used to teach reading at most schools, if the student cannot learn by the prescribed method, then there is something wrong with the student—not the method; and (4) extrinsic rewards are used to motivate young readers instead of using intrinsic motivation. A change is needed because children are failing, being labeled as slow readers, reading two and three grade levels below their age, and being retained because of failing reading scores. A successful approach to teaching reading will enable all students to be successful academically and thereby happier and better adjusted psychologically.

## Correcting At-Risk Problems in the Schools

A well-designed, well-implemented program can make the difference between offering true success or a well-intentioned but ineffective program. If we care about our children and youth, then we owe it to them to change how we teach and provide counseling in the schools because the approach we use in schools today will affect mental health and wellness for the remainder of life.

## Real-World Applications

### *Observational Extensions*

Go to the classroom, if possible, and observe the students who you wish to include in your new group.

- How do these students interact with the teacher and with their peers in the classroom?
- What needs do your group members display in the classroom?

• How will you change the learning environment in your new group intervention to enable these students to learn effectively?


## Troubleshooting Checklists for Organizing a New Group

1. How will you adjust for diversity among the members of your group?
2. Are there language barriers or cultural differences?
3. Are special needs accommodated?


## A Ready-to-Use Group-Centered Intervention: "Captain A and His Hot Air Balloon"

**Age level:** Kindergarten through 2nd Grade
**Learning Objective:** To increase word recognition skills for the letter A through hands-on activities.
**Counseling Objective:** To rebuild self-efficacy by teaching the beginning word decoding skills necessary to learn to read.
**Time needed:** 2 hours

*Tips for Using this Group-Centered Intervention*:  This group-centered intervention works well with children, kindergarten through second grade, or any at-risk children reading at the first grade level. This is a great hands-on group intervention which helps children who struggle to learn and understand the many phonetic sounds of the letter A. This group-centered intervention illustrates *vowel clustering* (Clanton Harpine 2010b) and how vowel clustering teaches a vowel sound. Please note that we are only including *a* sounds for the letter A with this exercise. AL, AU, AW, and other sounds used by the letter A are not included. We are clustering vowels together by sound, not letter.

*How to Expand into a Group-Centered Prevention Program*:  You can expand this intervention by substituting any vowel sound into the same activity (Captain E, Captain I, etc.) and clustering vowel sounds (Clanton Harpine 2010b). The initial activity takes approximately 2 hours, but can be expanded by repeating the intervention with different vowel clustered sounds into a month-long prevention program stressing vowel sounds. You may keep the hot air balloons posted on the wall or bulletin board for review and as a reminder of how vowel sounds are not always comprised from the same letters or letter combinations. If children meet only once a week, use a different vowel sound each week.

*Supplies Needed*:  construction paper, 1-in. wide colorful paper strips (thin photocopy paper curls easier; pre-cut if desired – 10 strips per student), yarn, scissors, pencils, crayons or markers, hole punch, and a picture of a hot air balloon if desired.

1. Ask children to describe a hot air balloon or show a picture of a hot air balloon to the children. Then, have children draw a large hot air balloon on their paper or have hot air balloon pictures prepared ahead of time [You may make a pattern for younger children to trace or photocopy balloon pictures]. Have each child decorate their hot air balloon.

2. Have children cut a square from brown construction paper to make a basket for their hot air balloon. This is Captain A's balloon. Have children draw a picture of Captain A to place in the basket of their balloon. Punch holes with a hole punch and attach the basket to the balloon with yarn. Make sure the basket dangles and sways back and forth.

3. Explain that a hot air balloon may use sand bags to help it stay anchored on the ground. Explain that, "we're going to make letter strips to help anchor Captain A and his hot air balloon." For very young children, you may want to have the children write or copy only one word on each strip. If your idea is to introduce the sound, then one word is adequate. If you want to increase vocabulary and use of words, then have older children write as many words as possible on their strips. Copying words from the board can be effective if student spelling skills are weak. It is much better to copy a word correctly than to write it incorrectly. Spelling the word correctly is important. The idea is to match words to a letter sound. You will need 10 strips of paper for each student.

4. Start with the ă sound, as in *at*. Have the children practice the ă sound. Give each child a strip of paper. Say: "Make a letter strip with as many words as possible using the ă sound, such as at, bat, map, fan, trap. Write short ă sound at the top of the strip. Then, fill the strip with words." If students are too young to spell, write words on the board and have them copy words as you review each word.

5. Then tell students: "The short ă sound can be changed into the long ā sound by adding *silent e* to certain words. Make a second sand bag strip changing words from the short ă sound to long ā sound by simply adding *silent e*. Example: fat to fate; fad, to fade; hat to hate; rat to rate. Write *silent e* at the top of the strip. Can you think of enough words to fill the entire strip? Never fear, there are many words that use *silent e*. Finish the strip with other words that do not have a short ă sound base but simply use the long ā sound by adding *silent e*: cake, bake, rake."

6. Give students a third strip of paper, then say: "You can also change short ă sound to long ā sound with AI. The I becomes silent. Example: man to main or ran to rain. Take a third letter strip. Write AI at the top of the strip and see how many AI words you can create. Remember, there are also words which use the AI sound which do not have a short ă *sound* base but simply use the long ā sound. Example: train, grain, stain."

7. On the fourth strip of paper, have students write AY. "When the long $\bar{a}$ sound appears at the end of a word, it is written as AY. The Y is silent, as in the words: bray, day, hay, say. Make a colorful word strip of AY words. Can you fill the entire strip?"

8. Remind students: "We must remember that word sounds can sometimes be tricky. AI and AY do not always have a long $\bar{a}$ sound. For example, the word kayak. The AY uses the $I$ sound, so, be careful of tricky words."

9. Give students a fifth strip and say: "What about EI? Can E and I be combined to form the long $\bar{a}$ sound? Yes, such as with the words: rein, freight, neighbor, reindeer. Take a word strip and see if you can think of more EI words? Be careful, EI can also use the sound for I." (For young children, you may want to spell EI words on the board and have them copy words.)

10. On the sixth strip: "At the end of a word, use the EY combination, as with: obey or they. List as many words as you can remember. EI and EY are tricky. AI, AY, EI and EY can also use other vowel sounds; so, be careful. Sound the words out carefully and listen for that long $\bar{a}$ sound."

11. On a seventh strip of paper, have students write EA and say: "E and A combine together to use the long $\bar{a}$ sound, as in the word: steak. But you want to watch out for the EA combination, because EA can also use the vowel sound for the letter E, as with: eat. Make a strip of EA words for the long $\bar{a}$ sound. How many can you think of?"

12. Have students make an eighth strip by saying: "EIGH uses the long $\bar{a}$ sound, as in: sleigh. Add the letter T to EIGH and you still have the long $\bar{a}$ sound, as in: eight. Make a word strip for words using the EIGH sound for the long $\bar{a}$ sound. EIGH is tricky too because EIGH can also be used for I as with: height. So be careful; words are tricky. Remember to use a dictionary if you need help."

13. On the ninth strip, have students write: "When A combines with the letter R, the letter R takes control of the word and changes the sound of A, as in car. The A is silent; R is the only sound you hear. Try these words: far, large, star, tar. Make a word strip. How many words can you add to your strip?"

14. On the tenth strip, have students write: air. "When A and R are combined with a second vowel, such as in air, the sound changes again. Try these words: air, bare, care, fair, mare, pair, stairs, stare, wear. Make a word strip for Captain A using the air sound."

15. Each student should have 10 strips of paper. Review strips to make sure everyone understands each sound correctly. Do not glue strips yet. The children will glue each strip to the hot air balloon basket as you read the story, just the top tip of the strip needs to be glued on. Let the strips dangle out of the basket. Instruct the students to "Listen to Captain A's story and curl the correct strip on a pencil when Captain A calls for each letter to be raised for take-off." Demonstrate how to curl strips on a pencil. If the students curl the strips tightly, thin strips will stay curled up in the basket at the end of the story as the students launch their balloons. Read the story as children curl and glue each strip in keeping with the story.

**Story**

Captain A and His Hot Air Balloon

Welcome friends. It's a wonderful day for a ride in my hot air balloon. Usually, I have lots of helpers, but today, I seem to be a bit shorthanded. Perhaps you will help? You see, because I'm Captain A, I have to make sure that I take all of the sounds for the letter A with me wherever I go. So, I have to check each sandbag, letter strip before I launch.

Let's start with the ă sound, as in *at*. We all know this sound. We find it in such words as cat, fat, rat, that. Check your letter strips. Find the strip for the short ă sound. Check your words, do you have only short ă sound words on your strip? Make sure that you have only short ă sound words because we do not have room for any extra passengers. If you're set, then take your pencil and curl the short ă sound strip tightly around your pencil. Glue just the top of your strip to the basket on your hot air balloon. We're getting ready to go. [Make sure everyone understands and has the task completed before you go to the next sound.]

Next, let's look for words which use the long ā sound by adding *silent e*, such as rate, cake, bake. Your letter strip should say *silent e* at the top. *Silent e* always makes the letter A say its name or use the long ā sound. Check your words, do you have only long ā sound words on your strip? Make sure that you have only long ā sound words which use *silent e* because we are going to be tight on space today. If your strip is ready, take your pencil and curl the long ā sound words which use *silent e* tightly around your pencil. Glue just the top of your strip to the basket on your hot air balloon. The way we're going we'll be in the air in no time. [Make sure everyone understands and has the task completed before you go to the next sound.]

There are seven different ways to make the long ā sound. Adding *silent e* is only one of the ways we have to make words use the long ā sound. For our next sandbag, look for the letter strip with AI written at the top. Words such as train and brain use the long ā sound with AI. Find the strip for the long ā sound with AI. Check your words, do you have only long ā sound with AI words on your strip? Make sure that you have only the long ā sound with AI words. If so, take your pencil and curl the long ā sound with AI strip tightly around your pencil. Glue just the top of your strip to the basket on your hot air balloon. You should now have three sandbag letter strips curled and ready to go. [Make sure everyone understands and has the task completed before you go to the next sound.]

Remember, there are seven different ways to make the long ā sound. AI and *silent e* are the first two ways. Now, let's add another way to make the long ā sound. Look for a strip marked AY at the top. When Y follows A, the Y is silent. AY is typically used at the end of a word, such as with: day, tray, say. Look for the letter strip with AY written at the top. Check your words, do you have only long ā sound with AY words on your strip? Make sure that you have only the long ā sound with AY words because we are running out of room and we do not have room for any extra passengers. Take your pencil and curl the long ā sound with AY strip tightly around your pencil. Glue just the top of your strip to the basket on your hot air balloon. You should now have four sandbag letter strips curled and ready to go. [Make sure everyone understands and has the task completed before you go to the next sound.]

We have AI, AY, and *silent e*. We now add: EI? When E and I are combined they can use the long *ā* sound but be careful because EI can also use the long I sound. So check your letter strip carefully. Make sure that you have included only EI words which use the long *ā* sound, such as: rein, feign. Look for the letter strip with EI written at the top. Check your words, do you have only long *ā* sound with EI words on your strip? Make sure that you have only the long *ā* sound with EI words because we are really running out of room. Take your pencil and curl the long *ā* sound with EI strip tightly around your pencil. Glue just the top of your strip to the basket on your hot air balloon. You should now have five sandbag letter strips curled and ready to go. [Make sure everyone understands and has the task completed before you go to the next sound.]

So far, for the long *ā* sound, we have AI, AY, EI, and *silent e*. We now add: EY, as with: obey or they. EI and EY are tricky. EI and EY can also use other vowel sounds. So, be careful. You want to add only EY words which use the long *ā* sound. Once you are certain you have only EY words on your strip, take your pencil and curl the long *ā* sound with EY strip tightly around your pencil. Glue just the top of your strip to the basket on your hot air balloon. You should now have six sandbag letter strips curled and ready to go. [Make sure everyone understands and has the task completed before you go to the next sound.]

For the long *ā* sound, we have AI, AY, EI, EY, and *silent e*. We now add: EA. E and A combine together to use the long *ā* sound, as in the word: steak. Be careful, though, because EA can also use the long E sound. Check your word strip carefully. Make sure that you have only EA words which use the long *ā* sound. Then, take your pencil and curl the long *ā sound* with EA strip tightly around your pencil. Glue just the top of your strip to the basket on your hot air balloon. Squish everyone together because we still have more sounds to come. You should now have seven sandbag letter strips curled and ready to go. [Make sure everyone understands and has the task completed before you go to the next sound.]

There is one more vowel combination which uses the long *ā* sound. It is EIGH, as in: sleigh. Add the letter T to EIGH and you still have the long *ā* sound, as in: eight. Look for the letter strip labeled EIGH. Check your word strip carefully. Make sure that you have only EIGH words which use the long *ā* sound. Then, take your pencil and curl the EIGH strip tightly around your pencil. Glue, just the top, of your strip to the basket on your hot air balloon. Make room; we still have more sounds coming. You should now have eight sandbag letter strips curled and ready to go. [Make sure everyone understands and has the task completed before you go to the next sound.]

Hold on, we're almost ready to launch our balloons. We have two sounds remaining. When A combines with the letter R, the letter R takes control of the word and changes the sound of A, as in *car*. The A is silent; R is the only sound you hear. So, look for the AR letter strip. Make sure that you have only AR words which have the *silent a* sound, as in car. There are two sounds with A and R; so be careful. Then, take your pencil and curl the AR strip tightly around your pencil.

Glue just the top of your strip to the basket on your hot air balloon. Leave room for one more strip. You should now have nine sandbag letter strips curled and ready to go. [Make sure everyone understands and has the task completed before you go to the next sound.]

When A and R are combined with a second vowel, such as in *air*, the sound changes again, as in: air, care, fair. Look for the AIR letter strip. Make sure that you have only AR words which combine with a second vowel for the *air* sound, as in stare. There are two sounds with A and R; so be careful. Then, take your pencil and curl the AIR strip tightly around your pencil. Glue just the top of your strip to the basket on your hot air balloon. We're finally ready to go.

Lift your balloon slowly off the ground. Hot air balloons never move fast. They are slow and graceful, so lift your balloon up into the air gently. Have a great flight and thanks for flying along with me.

# Chapter 3
# Organizing a New Group

*He was 6 years old, timid and shy, but a very cooperative little boy who had been retained because of his inability to memorize weekly word lists. The mother said, "I do not understand why he's having so much trouble; his sister did fine." Two weeks into the Reading Orienteering Club program, the little boy went home reading a vowel clustered story, incorporating eight new words. The little boy was so excited that he insisted on reading the story twice to his dad before going to bed. The dad remarked, "It's about time he decided to learn to read. I knew he could if he would just try."*

All too often, we as adults blame children when they fail to learn. The little boy's problem was not that he did not want to learn to read; he simply could not learn with the method being taught at his school. Children are individuals. Because we know that no two children learn in the exact same way, not even identical twins, and that a learning strategy that works for one child may not work for another, we must offer programs which allow all children to find success. We must see group members as individual contributors to a group, not just as a group of students. Every single member of a group has a unique, individual need and also has a special contribution to make to the group. Consider the strengths and weaknesses of each group member as you design your program.

## Underlying Principles of an Effective Group-Centered Prevention Program

Group-centered prevention programs are built upon a theoretical base utilizing self-efficacy, intrinsic motivation, and group cohesion (Clanton Harpine 2008). The intervention may last 1 hour, 1 week, over the summer, or all year; the process is still the same.

With the *school-based mental health approach,* the word "prevention" encompasses both correcting academic failure by rebuilding self-efficacy and also preventing future failure. Some students may need only a week-long motivational prevention program in order to review the necessary skills to enable them to be successful in the classroom. Such skill-building coupled with intrinsic motivation may provide

Clanton Harpine, *Group-Centered Prevention Programs for At-Risk Students,*
DOI 10.1007/978-1-4419-7248-4_3, © Springer Science+Business Media, LLC 2011

the structure for your prevention program. On the other hand, some students may need more intensive remedial skill-building through a program which is longer than merely 1 week. Design your program to meet the needs of the participants.

You may also be designing a more generalized program to be used with multiple groups, such as a program for all third graders. If you do not have a specific group of students in mind, then design for the general characteristics of the age group with which you plan to work. The principles of design are the same. There are five guiding principles to follow with the *school-based mental health approach* in organizing a new group-centered prevention program.

**Rule #1:** *Organize groups so that they support both academic and psychological development.* An example comes from a very progressive school that is striving hard to attain mandated test scores. In their quest to increase mandated test scores, the school developed remedial classes for students falling below the designated test score level. This at first sounds like an excellent program, but, unfortunately, the school did not consider the psychological needs alongside the academic needs of the student. A young middle school youth who was having trouble in both math and reading and barely passed at the end of the year was placed in these newly organized remedial classes. The student was pulled out of one of her favorite classes, which happened to be orchestra, for placement in the remedial program. At first we might say that academic needs should overshadow elective classes such as orchestra, but, then again, the psychological needs of the student must also be considered. That particular student excelled in orchestra; it was actually the only class that she excelled in. She loved the program and had earned the privilege of playing in the honors orchestra at her school. This orchestra had won many awards, competing even against high school orchestras, and the orchestra teacher was not considered an easy teacher. It was a top orchestra, and the teacher was very demanding. The teacher had learned that the student occasionally needed one-on-one assistance in order to learn new concepts. The teacher would take the student aside to teach her the concept; the student was then able to pick up and continue along with the rest of the orchestra group. By removing the student from orchestra, the school deprived the student of the opportunity to excel in school, to be a participant in one of the top programs the school offered. Every student needs to excel in at least one subject or one skill area to believe that it is possible to excel in others.

When we develop new groups, we must make certain that we balance academic and psychological needs. The student desperately needed to stay in orchestra, to be a member of a positive quality peer group, to succeed with a difficult teacher, and to see herself as being successful in at least one subject. Therefore, how we schedule new groups is very important. Will group time interfere with or take the student away from another needed activity? Psychological needs are just as important as academic needs.

**Rule #2:** *The setting is critical to the success of any group.* When I first started working with the 15-year-old teen mentioned in Chapter 2, I do not think she would ever have consented to reading tutoring if I had approached her as an individual. She was embarrassed that she could not read and did not want any of her friends to find out. Because she had been recruited as part of a small group, she did not feel singled out. All three of the teens were working on improving reading skills. Each of the three teenagers read at a different reading level; therefore, we essentially conducted one-on-one tutoring in a group setting. The advantage was that meeting in the same room at the same time for similar skills training reduced the feelings of inadequacy and failure. Her feeling was that everyone's working; I'm not the only one who needs help.

While some students need one-on-one instruction, I still believe that the group setting has merits over individual pull-out tutoring. The university students left campus for summer break at the end of the semester and I was only able to continue working with the 15-year-old, who I thought needed the most help. She was very reluctant to be seen going to tutoring alone. We needed to change rooms and found ourselves tucked in the back of the clothing distribution room at the community center so that her fear of being seen by other teens would not prevent her from coming to the tutoring sessions. Her desire to read was still just as strong as it had always been, but her fear of others discovering that she could not read almost prevented her from continuing. There is comfort in numbers, but not just any group will do. Groups must be organized very carefully.

**Rule #3:** *The group must meet the needs of the participants.* The group that I organized for the three teens differed from most group prevention programs. Most group-centered programs that I design involve group interaction, hands-on learning techniques, and learning centers. Yet this teenage reading group needed more one-on-one instruction because of their differences in reading abilities. They were not able to learn as a group, but they desperately needed a group setting and the support of a positive peer group in order to be willing to risk participating in tutoring. Therefore, when we organize new groups, we must look at the needs of the group members. Students will not learn in a group setting in which they do not experience some degree of interpersonal satisfaction. Satisfaction comes from improved self-efficacy (success in accomplishing a task or learning classroom material which has previously proved impossible) and positive peer relationships with other group members.

Although schools and many academic programs stress self-esteem, self-esteem is only a judgment of self-worth, of like or dislike (Swann et al. 2007). A student may feel accepted by a peer group, or be proud of group membership, and still fail every single subject. Self-esteem does not necessarily lead to change or positive psychological development. Self-efficacy, on the other hand, is a judgment of ability, the perception and belief that a person can accomplish a specified task (Bandura 1977). Self-efficacy affects how well students apply the skills and knowledge they have attained, while generating persistence and willingness to work on difficult tasks. Self-efficacy, then, is the catalyst for change that is missing in school-based interventions.

Self-efficacy, unlike pure social emotional programming, is linked to the central mission of the school in that self-efficacy addresses both the academic and mental health needs of the students. By strengthening self-efficacy through prevention programming, we will strengthen both academic competence and well being.

**Rule #4:** *Teaching methods must support healthy psychological development.* The methods that we use to teach can either help or hinder psychological development. An example comes from a family with six children, which was a well-educated, middle-class, two-parent family. The parents were involved at school and in community activities with their children. All six children were bright and usually ranked among the top students in their class. The mother, who knew that I worked with at-risk readers, approached me one day most upset that her two youngest children were struggling with reading. She said, "I have to fight with them just to get them to read, anything. The others always loved reading." All of her children had gone to the same school, even had some of the same teachers, but the school had changed to a whole language program with the last two children. I suggested that she teach phonics to her two youngest children at home and gave her copies of some of the *vowel clustering* curriculum (Clanton Harpine 2010b) I was working with. A few months later, she called me and said, "I can't get them to stop reading; everywhere they go they take a book, and they are so much happier. They're not even angry about going to school anymore." The curriculum and teaching methods that schools use in the classroom directly influence psychological development. When we create school-based group-centered prevention programs, we must incorporate teaching methods that will support positive psychological development.

Students learn more and better retain what they learn when they are actively engaged in the learning process (Deci and Ryan 1985). This holds for short-term mastery, long-term retention, and overall understanding of concepts. Critical thinking improves when teachers make the most of interactive student discussions, teach problem-solving, and allow students to apply what is being learned to real-life situations. Group discussions and problem-solving have the greatest impact on critical thinking and enhance student performance on examinations. By thinking critically, students learn how to evaluate and analyze information. Critical thinking questions employ a higher level of cognitive processing and require analysis, comparison, contrast, evaluation, and sometimes even prediction of consequences (Hertz-Lazarowitz 1992). Critical thinking provides students with a deeper understanding than simply memorizing facts (Webb 1992). Problem-solving techniques improve the understanding of textbook material, and, when students are required to apply theories from the textbook to real-life situations, long-term, life-long learning is strengthened.

**Rule #5:** *Cohesive groups are more successful.* A successful group program must include motivation for change. This is often best achieved when students believe that the group will help them. A supportive, cohesive group sets the atmosphere for change. A student's behavior in a new group is often influenced by the way the group is structured. Competition destroys group cohesion and reduces intrinsic motivation because at-risk students perceive their self-worth from the approval of others (Ryan and Deci 2000). Social feedback then becomes a judgment. Students who struggle in the classroom have an enhanced sensitivity to evaluation. They are also more concerned about their self-worth and are typically more critical in their self-evaluations. When we organize new groups, we must develop group interventions which meet both the psychological and academic needs of the students in positive peer group settings which stress group cohesion.

## Developing Effective Prevention Programs

In designing an effective prevention program, we must incorporate counseling, intrinsic motivation, and skill building. It is not enough to teach skills, conduct therapy, or motivate. There must be a combination. The combination is what makes group-centered prevention programming successful. Each program will be different and must be designed around the educational and psychological needs of the students in your group.

The focus in this book is on designing group-centered prevention programs, particularly week-long preventive group-centered programs. As you develop your program design, how will you incorporate learning and counseling in your program?

*Incorporating counseling.* For children to succeed in the classroom, they must be motivated to learn. To feel motivated, children must experience self-determination. Self-determination is the freedom to choose to learn rather than being forced to do so (Deci et al. 1995). Children learn for the pleasure of learning or the desire to acquire knowledge. Learning for the thrill of learning or to satisfy an intrinsic need for inquiry does not happen in forced educational settings. *Camp Sharigan* uses hands-on intrinsic motivators because intrinsic motivation is superior to extrinsic motivation. Children have a natural desire to be competent and succeed at school (Vallerand et al. 1997).

*Incorporating learning.* As you plan your program, do not plan mere extensions of the classroom or workbook sessions. If children are failing in the classroom, they will fail when you give them the same workbook pages in your program. Repetition of the same unsuccessful teaching methods will not cause at-risk readers to read. More practice and more workbook pages are not the answer to the problem. Each time the child fails, self-confidence is lowered. Skill-building is essential for change, so use a new approach, a hands-on teaching approach. All children, but especially at-risk children, learn by doing. For your program to be effective, it must incorporate a new way of learning.

*Incorporating change into your program.* An effective program is one that helps the individual change. This may be a change in how the student thinks or a change in how the student acts. Either way, the change is internalized and becomes a part of the student's perceived self-concept. Most remedial, tutorial pull-out, or after-school programs function as extensions of the traditional school day. Worksheets, reading groups, and tutoring fail to solve the real problem.

An example comes from an after-school homework program to which I take my university students periodically in order to give them field experience working with at-risk children. On that particular day, I had taken a class of 20 university students to work one-on-one to help children complete their homework. One university student brought a stapled stack of 14 workbook pages to me saying, "I can't get the little girl to do her homework." The little girl in question was a second grader who sat with tears streaming down her face saying, "I have to get it all done or I'll get in trouble." When I sat down to work with the little girl, it became obvious that the little girl did not know how to complete any of the workbook pages. When I retaught the concepts covered on a page, she could then complete the page, but it was not possible to reteach 14 different workbook pages in the 1-hour homework session. The child was not refusing to do her homework, she could not do her homework because she didn't know how to do it. Workbook pages do not teach, nor do stickers or threats of punishment. Programs based on such practices are doomed to failure.

*Combining counseling and skills training.* Prevention programs that incorporate both motivational skill building and counseling can be set up within our current public school system. Many schools offer an after-school program for at-risk readers, but utilize the same teaching strategies under which the child failed to learn to read in the classroom. What is needed is a totally different approach to learning: *the school-based mental health approach.* When such an approach is used, as with *Camp Sharigan* and the *Reading Orienteering Club,* then children have the opportunity to relearn without the stigmatization of previous failure. Group-centered prevention programs such as *Camp Sharigan* teach by combining counseling and remedial skill building. With reading, the change becomes a part of how children perceive themselves as being able to read. If students think they can read, then they will work harder to strive to read. If students think that they cannot read or do not read as well as other children in the class, then they will be reluctant to try, and failure will result.

We often think reading is merely an elementary school problem. Not so. There are many middle school and high school students who cannot read at grade level. On the Nation's Report Card in 2009, it was reported that 50% of high school students cannot read at grade level, that 90% of students who drop out of school cannot read at grade level, and that reading problems may be one of the leading causes motivating students to drop out (NAEP 2009). Reading failure contributes to failure in math, social studies, science, and every endeavor which requires the student to read.

## Designing a Group-Centered Program Packet

Effective prevention programming must speak directly to the psychological needs of at-risk students. Combining therapy and learning together in the same program makes this possible. The advantage of incorporating therapy and learning into the same program is that struggling at-risk children learn to be successful in a classroom atmosphere. Failure is erased; self-efficacy restored.

## *Step 3: Proposed Change*

What change do you propose? How do you plan to implement this change? Explain how your proposal will alleviate the causes of the problem or need.

How will the group react to your proposed program of change? Remember that group members function as a total cohesive group or as subgroups. (A program of change will affect everyone in the group. You must think of the entire group as you plan.)

How will you measure improvement or change with your program? Will the individual group be able to notice change on a daily or weekly basis?

What are the advantages of your program? What are the disadvantages? Can you reduce or eliminate the disadvantages? If you cannot eliminate a disadvantage, can you minimize its affect?

What will you do if the group does not comply or show positive results from your program? How will you adapt?

For the design example to Step 3, I have presented my response in the Design Example as if I were answering the questions, just as you have done in your design process. With reading failure, at-risk children need to improve reading scores in order to prevent psychological distress from a perceived sense of failure. The *Camp Sharigan* program is one example. Children participating in *Camp Sharigan* have repeatedly outscored other children on tests conducted on the program (Clanton Harpine 2005a, 2007a; Clanton Harpine and Reid 2009a, b). Hands-on interactive group-centered teaching methods and intrinsic skill-building learning center activities are integral to the success of the *Camp Sharigan* approach (Clanton Harpine 2008). *Camp Sharigan* combines learning and counseling through academic remedial reading training in a group-centered hands-on motivational prevention program. My design examples explain these hands-on concepts.

At this point, you are just beginning to develop your program ideas; you will not have a complete program formulated. That will be our job throughout the remainder of the book. For Design Step 3, write down what you want your program to accomplish. We will work on implementation of your ideas in later chapters.


**Step 3, Design Example**

I propose to offer a group program which will help children learn to read. I also propose to offer a group program which will help children learn social skills so that they can be successful in the classroom and in life. I want a program that focuses both on the academic and psychological needs of my group.

*To implement change.* I want a fun atmosphere which will help the children forget that reading is a school subject that they do not like. Instead, I want the children to think of reading as being fun, something they would rather do than watch television. Because one of the major goals is motivation, a week-long format to intensify the excitement and motivation will be used.

*To erase the cause of the problem.* Hands-on learning techniques will be stressed because students learn best through active involvement. Students may range in reading ability from being able to read only a few words to children who read at the third grade level. Therefore, the program must incorporate a high degree of individualized instruction, but I still want the therapeutic power of group process in the program. Students are most likely not accustomed to working in small groups or experienced with employing critical thinking.

*Measuring improvement.* Ongoing progress will be measured by monitoring reading improvement. Monitoring stories and sight words will allow each child to read at their grade level and see continuous improvement throughout the week. If a child does not show improvement, a volunteer tutor will be assigned to provide more one-on-one assistance and individualized instruction.

*Advantages of this type of program.* Research shows that students learn more and are more likely to retain what they learn when they are actively engaged in the learning process. Hands-on activities provide this engagement. Hands-on activities will be used because hands-on activities can be intrinsically motivating and instructional.

The counseling aspect of the program is built into the cohesive group structure and the intrinsic motivators that I plan to use. The instructional portion of the program will focus on reading skills. Bandura (1977) stated that it is not possible to rebuild self-efficacy without skill-building; we must teach the necessary skills if we are to rebuild a student's belief that they can succeed in the classroom. Skill-building is essential for change. I'll balance the need for skills and the need for counseling through hands-on learning strategies which incorporate individualized instruction in an intrinsically motivational cohesive group structure.

*Disadvantages.*  At this point in the planning process, I see two disadvantages: (1) I need to recruit volunteers to work one-on-one with the children at each learning center and (2) I need to invest time and effort into creating a fun atmosphere. To minimize these disadvantages, I can solicit volunteer help from a variety of university and community groups. Because I am creating program packets, I will only have the expenditure of time for creating the program at the beginning.

*Adapting to student needs.*  I want to remain flexible to student needs. I will monitor student progress throughout the week. I'll use reading lists to measure progress on a daily basis.

## Designing a Program of Change

At this point, as you work through the steps and plan your program design, you should have a sketched-out idea of what you want your program to resemble. This is by no means a completed program plan. Next, we want to take our sketch from Step 3 and begin to mold and shape our programming ideas into an effective program.

Two questions to ask yourself at this point in the design process: (1) Am I using the same old techniques from the classroom or have I proposed new, exciting intrinsic learning techniques that will help at-risk children erase failure from the classroom? (2) Am I combining both counseling and learning in my program? If you cannot answer "yes" to both of these questions, return to your program design in Step 3 and implement changes.

## Real-World Applications

### *Observational Extensions*

Observe your group members during instruction in the subject you are incorporating into your group intervention. If you are using reading, observe reading; if using math, observe math.

- What problems do you see?
- How do your group members handle confusion or inability to understand a concept?
- What changes should you make to the learning environment to help these students become more successful?

## *Troubleshooting Checklists for Designing a New Group-Centered Program*

1. What are the advantages and disadvantages of the program you propose?
2. How can you eliminate or at least reduce the effect of such disadvantages?
3. What is the financial cost of your program? Will participants have to pay to attend? If so, will financial assistance be available?
4. Can the cost be reduced?
5. How will you justify the cost?

## *A Ready-to-Use Group-Centered Intervention: "Self-Reflection: Using a Narrative to Teach Writing Skills"*

**Age level:** High School
**Learning Objective:** To enhance writing skills through a reflective, critical thinking group activity.
**Counseling Objective:** To enhance the development of individual responsibility and to strengthen problem solving group skills.
**Time needed:** 1 or 2 hours (depending on whether the story is read as a group or as a homework assignment).

*Tips for using this group-centered intervention*: We have all struggled with the task of writing a research paper. As a teacher, even at the university level, I am constantly searching for new ways to introduce students to the intricacies of writing a well-organized research paper. Using a story is one approach for encouraging critical thinking and evaluation.

*How to expand into a group-centered prevention program*: This group-centered intervention can easily be expanded into a week-long or month-long research writing project. You can use small group peer evaluations to help students find problems. For example, use each of the warning statements, have groups either search for that problem in their own writings or have students work with a partner and check each other's papers. Correcting writing style one step at a time is the best way to develop better writers. You can use the same process for grammar rules. Write a sheet of warning statements; have students search for corrections that need to be made.

*Supplies Needed*: Copy of the story for each student and a place where students can work as a small group

1. Assign the story before students begin writing their research papers. Have students read the story "*Self-Reflection*" either orally as a class or independently as homework. Students enjoy reading orally with one person reading for the narrator and a second deep or stern voice for the warning signs, with other readers filling in by reading the research sections. Reading as a group can be fun.

2. In this short narrative, a student ponders the question of how to organize and write a research paper that does not border on plagiarism, read like a book report, or consist of a stream of never-ending quotations. As the student struggles through the writing process in dialog with herself, she illustrates many of the concerns, questions, and problems faced by students when confronted with the task of writing a research paper.

3. Sometimes a narrative can be used to teach hard-to-learn material better than lecture or direct instruction. The end of the story asks the reader(s) to develop an outline using the information contained in the story. Students can work together in groups to share ideas. Then, after students have practiced writing an outline for the narrator in the story, they can turn to their own research paper and apply the same rules.

4. This group-centered intervention can also be used for individual and group evaluation which encourages critical thinking. Students may also use this narrative with the bold-faced warning statements to evaluate their own research writing. Working in groups can help students learn to work together, strengthening the critical-thinking component of this intervention.

5. Assignment (Story to be read either in class or individually.): "Read the following story entitled *Self-Reflection*. This story illustrates the frustrations of a student as she sits down the night before to write her research paper. As the student struggles to write, she encounters many warnings from her teacher on the assignment sheet."

6. Group Assignment to Enhance Critical Thinking (To be used after students have read the story.): "Developing main ideas to fit a thesis statement can often be tricky. Can you help the student in our story write three main ideas to fit her thesis statement? Using the research included in the story, how would you develop these three main ideas in the outline? Does the student have enough research to support her thesis? If you decide that the student needs more research, what does the student need?"

## Story

### Self-Reflection

I have been staring at this computer screen for 3 solid hours and I have written exactly one word. Take that back, two words: "Reading is..." After all, "is" constitutes a word. Yes, I know I shouldn't have put this paper off till tonight, but I've been so busy and anyway who wants to write about reading? I don't know why my teacher gave me this topic. Yes I know, I said that I couldn't think of anything to research; I'll never make that mistake again.

I found tons of information on the Internet, and I even read the stack of articles Mrs. Gordon gave me in class, but I have no idea what I want to write. Let's see,


*Reading Failure Causes Students to Drop Out of School*

*Imagine how hard it would be to sit in a classroom day after day trying to read if you were convinced beforehand that you would never be able to do so. Many children cannot read and are convinced that they will never learn to read. Reading failure can have damaging effects throughout life and even lead to dropping out of school before graduation.*

*Reading failure is a major problem facing our country today. We must find a way to help children learn to read before it is too late.*


That's not so bad, but I've said everything I had to say. I've only written two short paragraphs. Where's my assignment sheet? I'm certain this paper has to be longer than two paragraphs. What's this? Mrs. Gordon has printed a long list of warnings on our assignment sheet.

**WARNING #1:  DID YOU CITE SOURCES CORRECTLY? WHEN QUOTING OR USING THE IDEAS OF ANOTHER AUTHOR, YOU MUST GIVE CREDIT TO THE ORIGINAL AUTHOR. ONE RULE TO FOLLOW IS: DID YOU KNOW THE INFORMATION BEFORE YOU READ THE REFERENCE? IF YOU LEARNED THE INFORMATION THAT YOU ARE NOW WRITING IN YOUR RESEARCH PAPER FROM YOUR REFERENCES, YOU MUST CITE THE REFERENCES AND GIVE CREDIT TO THE AUTHORS OF YOUR REFERENCE MATERIAL. OTHERWISE YOU ARE GUILTY OF PLAGIARISM – STEALING SOMEONE ELSE'S WORDS OR IDEAS AND USING THEM AS YOUR OWN.**

No, stop, I'm not a thief. I didn't steal anything. Well, I mean; I guess it's true that I didn't know that reading failure can cause people to drop out of school. I guess I never even thought about kids not being able to read. I mean, I know some people struggle more than others. So I guess you could say I learned the things I wrote in my paper from reading all that stuff on-line and from those articles Mrs. Gordon gave me. Oh, no, I'm really in trouble; I've committed plagiarism. I'm a thief. Maybe, I can just put a little author thing at the end of each paragraph.

**WARNING #2: YOU CANNOT SIMPLY PLACE A CITATION AT THE END OF THE PARAGRAPH AND SAY THAT IT COVERS THE ENTIRE PARAGRAPH. YOU MUST CITE EACH SENTENCE INDIVIDUALLY.**

Wonderful, I'll be at this all night. Oh wait, maybe not. I'll use this. This should fix it; I've cited everything.

*"Reading failure is like the domino effect. Once a child falls behind, failure in reading begins to seep into every crevice of the educational process" (Clanton Harpine 2008, p. 55). "When children lose the ability to cope with the pressures of the classroom and with peer pressure from friends, they no longer perceive that they have the ability to control their environment or to recover from setbacks, poor grades, or difficult situations in the classroom" (Clanton Harpine 2008, p. 3). "Poor readers struggle to write, cannot read their social studies or science text, have difficulty with story problems in math, and do not volunteer to participate in any activities that require reading" (Clanton Harpine 2008, p. 55). "Because reading is so closely intertwined with our self-identity and early development, the methods that we use in teaching children to read become an integral component of school-based mental health. What happens in the classroom has a direct effect on the child's psychological well-being today and throughout life" (Clanton Harpine 2008, pp. 56–57).*

Wow! Look how nicely I made all of those quotes fit together. This is going to be a great paper. It's easy too; you just make the quotes squish together. I'll be done in no time. How long did she say this paper has to be?

**WARNING #3: BE CAREFUL THAT YOU DO NOT SIMPLY STRING QUOTATIONS TOGETHER. ONE QUOTATION, FOLLOWED BY ANOTHER QUOTATION, FOLLOWED BY ANOTHER QUOTATION IS NOT RESEARCH WRITING. IT IS COPYING QUOTATIONS. USE QUOTATIONS SPARINGLY.**

I think I am beginning to feel the stress that author talked about. Let me see if I have this straight, (1) I can't read an article and then simply write down what I learned from that article and call it MY research paper, (2) I have to cite sources for everything and a single citation at the end of the paragraph does not cover everything discussed in the paragraph above, and if that's not bad enough, (3) I can't take a group of quotations from an author and string them together very cleverly into a paragraph and call that a research paper. Okay, I give up; exactly what is a research paper?

**WARNING #4: IN A RESEARCH PAPER, YOU WRITE YOUR OWN WORDS, CITING REFERENCES FOR NEW IDEAS AND INFORMATION LEARNED.**

Great, I'll be citing everything because I do not know anything about reading.

*Negative labels in the classroom are bad and create negative perceptions (Clanton Harpine 2008). Lack of skills can cause students to drop out of school before graduation (Clanton Harpine 2008). Reading failure is made worse because it happens in the public arena of a classroom (Clanton Harpine 2008). Students who struggle to read are more likely to be involved in school violence, bullying, and illegal substance use (Clanton Harpine 2008).*

**WARNING #5: WHEN PARAPHRASING, NEVER USE MORE THAN THREE WORDS FROM THE SOURCE THAT YOU ARE PARAPHRASING.**

**IF YOU USE MORE THAN THREE WORDS, QUOTE WORD FOR WORD AND USE QUOTATION MARKS.**

I should be OK on that warning. No, I use only two words in that sentence (negative perceptions – whatever that is), and three on that one (lack of skills), and two in the next paragraph (public arena – I have no idea what that is but it sounds good), and three in the last paragraph (illegal substance use). That looks fine. What's next?

**WARNING #6: BE CAREFUL NOT TO FALL INTO THE TRAP OF WRITING A BOOK/ARTICLE REPORT. CHECK YOUR PAPER. ARE YOU WRITING AN ENTIRE PARAGRAPH FROM ONE SOURCE? DO YOU FILL AN ENTIRE PAGE WITH REFERENCES FROM ONLY ONE SOURCE? IN THAT CASE, YOU ARE GIVING A REPORT ON WHAT AN AUTHOR SAID. REPORTING OR SUMMARIZING A BOOK OR ARTICLE IS NOT RESEARCH WRITING. RETURN TO YOUR OUTLINE. SEEK REFERENCES WHICH SUPPORT YOUR MAIN IDEAS. DO NOT SIMPLY REPORT ON THE RESEARCH YOU FOUND AND DO NOT SIMPLY SHAPE YOUR MAIN IDEAS TO FIT THE RESEARCH YOU HAVE FOUND. WRITE FROM YOUR OUTLINE.**

What outline? I don't remember anything about an outline. Oh that,

**TAKE YOUR RESEARCH QUESTION. DEVELOP A THESIS STATEMENT AND THREE MAIN IDEAS TO SUPPORT YOUR THESIS. THEN GO AND DO YOUR RESEARCH. REMEMBER TO USE YOUR OUTLINE TO ORGANIZE YOUR RESEARCH AND TO WRITE YOUR PAPER.**

Oh dear, I have to start over. My research question was: Does reading failure cause students to drop out of school before graduation? I decided that my thesis was: Reading failure causes students to drop out of school. That means my three main ideas are...

# Chapter 4
# Identifying the Needs of the Group

*He was a first grader, home schooled and not accustomed to working with other students in a group setting. He was very eager to learn and always cooperative. His primary problem was insecurity. He kept wanting to leave and be with his mother or older sister. When he wasn't feeling scared, his eagerness to work was very helpful because he attended a program in which most students displayed poor motivation and poor study skills. He was always eager to go to the next learning center and other students began to follow his example. The problem was to keep him busy so that he would not think about going home. With Camp Sharigan, he was fine because the pace was very fast, but he was also enrolled in the year-long Reading Orienteering Club program, which focuses more on remedial skills and uses a slower pace. This gave him more opportunities to think of mom. As the year progressed, he became more confident working in the group and did not always need reassurance that mom would return. While any group experience might have helped the little first grader learn to be more confident in a group setting, he showed others in the reading program not to give up so easily when challenged with a difficult task. He was an excellent role model. Some group members may give as much to the group as they receive.*

When organizing a new group, it is important to consider the group's composition. What is the group supposed to accomplish? Why are these group members in the same group?

Some group members have similar problems, but no two group members are exactly the same, nor can they be treated in exactly the same manner. Any program design must incorporate the individual needs of each participant and the needs of the total group as they work together.

One cannot simply gather students together, place them in a group, and hope that they will be successful. Just being a member of a group is not what makes groups successful. The programmer must design and build success into the group. The *school-based mental health approach* means that we look at the students' academic and psychological needs alike. An effective program cannot address just the group members' academic needs, nor can an effective school-based mental health program just address the students' psychological needs. Academic and psychological needs must be intertwined for the program to be effective

Clanton Harpine, *Group-Centered Prevention Programs for At-Risk Students*, DOI 10.1007/978-1-4419-7248-4_4, © Springer Science+Business Media, LLC 2011

(Greenberg et al. 2003). Needs may differ across the domains of group, school, and life. What a child needs to be successful in school may not be everything that is needed to succeed in life.

## Group Composition

It is also important to consider how the students in a group came together. Was the group advertised and does it include everyone who expressed an interest? Were you selective? It makes a difference. If students feel forced to participate in the group, intrinsic motivation is very low; therefore, one of the first tasks must be to increase intrinsic motivation and commitment to the group. If group members elected to join the group, then they are more committed and motivated to get involved.

The roles of parents and teachers in school-based mental health groups are also important. Do parents want their children to participate in your group? Are parents embarrassed that their children may need remedial help? Will parental embarrassment deter a child's participation?

I actually had a parent remove a child from my *Reading Orienteering Club* program because someone mentioned that it was a remedial program. If possible, I try to mix both strong and remedial readers together in the *Reading Orienteering Club* so that it is not just a program for students who cannot read at grade level. As mentioned in the opening example, highly motivated group members make excellent role models. Nonetheless, the mother was convinced that everyone would think her child could not read if she allowed her child to participate in the program. The child actually tested below grade level in reading and could have greatly improved through the program. The student's teacher recommended that the child participate. For the week and a half that the student was allowed to attend the program, the child made excellent progress and really enjoyed being in the group, but the child was forbidden to attend by the mother. Therefore, always be aware of parental fears.

When designing an effective group program, we need to know the individual needs of every group member. Were students recommended for the group by the classroom teacher because of problems in the classroom? What specific problems does each student bring to the group? What does each student need from the group? How will the group members blend together?

## Describing the Group

The best way to get to know your group is by writing a description of your group and listing the needs of each student. Analyze your group before you start designing your program. You want your program to meet the needs of your participants.

## *Step 4: Description of the Group*

Make a list of all group members.

(If you chose a group to work with in Chapter 2, then use that group. If you have not chosen a group, you need to identify a group to work with.)

Describe the individuals in the group (focus on interaction, personality, self-concept, and self-efficacy):

What does each student need (academically and psychologically) to be successful in the group?

What does each student need (academically and psychologically) to be successful in school?

What does each student need (academically and psychologically) to be successful in life?

**Step 4, Design Example**

My group example for Step 4 is an actual group that I worked with consisting of 20 children from a variety of schools. My group was pulled together from an open call to the community and area schools for children interested in participating in a reading program. The students were not selected by me, but I accepted every student who enrolled. Their abilities ranged from two children reading above their grade level, to 15 children reading one to two grade levels below their age. At least half of the students had been retained one year and many were failing reading when they entered the program. Others read at grade level but with little comprehension.

The group consisted of children aged from 5 to 11 years old, racially mixed, representing a spectrum of socioeconomic backgrounds ranging from the housing projects to middle-class suburbia. Some of the children spoke very loudly and had difficulty sitting down to work quietly. Four of the children had been diagnosed by their school as having attention deficit hyperactivity disorder (ADHD), two of which were on medication and two not taking medication. One child had been labeled both as having ADHD and a cognitive disorder.

Upon first observation, five of the children displayed behavior problems. These five students typically ran down the hall pushing and shoving, fighting over chairs, and engaging in any other disruptive behavior they could contrive. One student constantly belittled other children, making fun of those who could not read or who had trouble completing an assignment. In contrast, seven of the children were so quiet that they would not even talk. At the beginning, the 20 students did not interact or work well together. Their personalities differed too much. Yet this was a perfect group for a group-centered prevention program because it encompassed the mixture of personalities and interactive experiences found in a regular classroom.

*Student needs.* The students in this group need individual lessons based on their skill ability and cohesive group experiences that would transfer back to the classroom. The program design must fulfill both of these needs.

*Group needs.* Some children came from the same school or neighborhood; others did not know each other before beginning *Camp Sharigan*. The neighborhood and school groups tended to cluster together and reject participation by those "outside" the familiar school and neighborhood groupings. Teamwork and group cohesion would be a challenge.

*Classroom needs.* Eighteen of the 20 children considered themselves to be poor readers. Self-efficacy for the group as a whole was low and most of the children were convinced they would never be able to read. It should also be noted that many of the parents and classroom teachers did not think that it would be possible for the students to improve. Therefore, the program must include skill-building as a first priority. Only two children in the group had a positive attitude toward their ability to read.

Sometimes making a graph or chart can be helpful for comparing and contrasting the needs of your group members. If we look at the 20 students described in Step 4, we might compile the following chart. Because this was an actual group that I worked with, the students have been listed by number instead of by name.

| Stu # | Students having problems in reading | Students in Kindergarten or First Grade | Students who have been retained because of failing grades in reading | Diagnosed with ADHD or ADD | Students having problems in the classroom with social skills | Students with lack of confidence in reading |
|---|---|---|---|---|---|---|
| 1 | Yes | F | | ADHD/Med | Yes | Yes |
| 2 | Yes | F | | | Yes | Yes |
| 3 | Yes | | | | Yes | Yes |
| 4 | Yes | | R | | Yes | |
| 5 | | K | | | Yes | |
| 6 | Yes | | | ADHD | Yes | Yes |
| 7 | Yes | | | | Yes | Yes |
| 8 | Yes | F | | | Yes | Yes |
| 9 | Yes | | R | ADD | Yes | Yes |
| 10 | Yes | | R | ADHD/Med | Yes | Yes |
| 11 | | | | | Yes | |
| 12 | | | | | Yes | |
| 13 | Yes | F | | | Yes | Yes |
| 14 | Yes | | R | | Yes | Yes |
| 15 | | | | | Yes | |
| 16 | Yes | | R | ADHD | Yes | Yes |
| 17 | Yes | K | R | | Yes | Yes |
| 18 | Yes | | | | Yes | Yes |
| 19 | Yes | F | | | Yes | Yes |
| 20 | Yes | | R | | Yes | Yes |

*ADHD* attention deficit hyperactivity disorder, *ADD* attention deficit disorder

In schools, we often fall prey to technical reports or summaries. While a chart gives a nice overview of the group and the problems facing the group, it does not help us get acquainted with the group members as individuals. To develop an effective program, we must look at these students as individuals and not just as numbers on a page.

Write a brief description of each student. I give four examples from the chart which illustrate how helpful detailed descriptions can be. The student numbers listed correspond to the student number on the chart.

**Student #1**: He was an African-American first-grade student reading at the pre-primer level. He was from a low socioeconomic background and had not attended preschool or received any help in preparing to go to school. He had a speech problem, difficulty pronouncing words, and speaking. He also spoke very rapidly which made his speech harder to understand. He was sensitive about his speech problem because the children at school often teased him. He had been diagnosed by the school as having ADHD and placed on medication. He became bored very easily and frequently simply gave up and stopped trying, especially when reading. He desperately needed phonics training to help him hear and distinguish sounds so that he could improve his pronunciation skills. He needed to work on rebuilding his self-efficacy through structured skill building sessions. He also needed acceptance from the group, support, and a cohesive working environment. Modeling could be excellent for this student, especially if he could work with another student slightly above his reading level. I did not want him to have a partner who was too advanced because that would make him feel inferior, but at the same time, he needed a partner who would encourage him to keep working instead of giving up. For school, he needed the skills to succeed in the classroom: reading, writing, speaking, and social ability. For life, he needed to believe that he could learn to read. Being successful in the group might make a lifelong difference for this student.

**Student #6**: An African-American third-grade male student reading a little below grade level was enrolled in the group by his after-school counselor. He was very quiet, seemed to have a lot of difficulty working with others in a group, and he seemed unsure of himself. He was aggressive one minute and in tears the next. He needed acceptance from the group and at school, one and to learn how to work with others in a group setting. He knew four other students in the group from school, but he was not close friends with anyone attending the group. Academically, he needed to sharpen his skills to make him more confident, but his biggest problems lay with social skills. The challenge was going to be keeping him enrolled in the group; he had a tendency to withdraw from anything that was the least bit threatening. He simply gave up and quit. Sticking to a hard task without giving up would be his life skill to work on.

**Student #10**: An African-American third-grade student, already retained once, was being socially promoted by the school system because of reading failure. She presently read at the first grade level. Had been diagnosed with ADHD, was extremely loud and hyper, and had difficulty completing a task. She had given up; she thought she would never be able to learn to read. From the group, she needed skills training, particularly phonics, to improve her reading and writing skills. She needed a model for proper group behavior in the classroom, someone she could work with who would help her stop and think before acting out. The group would also be instrumental in helping her learn to believe in herself and also change how she approaches learning tasks. For school, she needed academic and social skills training to be successful in the classroom. For life, she needed to learn to read and believe in herself so that she can go out into the world and be successful.

**Student #14**: An African-American second-grade student was friends with four other students in the group and very reluctantly joined the group. He showed little interest in reading; he read at the first-grade level. Weak academic and group skills made it a challenge to work with this student. His mother did not see an advantage to having him learn to read; she did not feel reading was necessary. From the group, he needed motivation to change. Unless he could become motivated to change early in the group sessions, he would, most likely, drop out. He needed to see an immediate benefit from being in the group. His lack of motivation for school would be the first big hurdle with this student. He considered himself a failure and saw no reason to bother trying to learn. His sense of failure was reinforced by his mother and the school.

## Evaluating Group Needs

Two of the main challenges in working with the group I have identified in my design example would be to change their self-efficacy about reading and to generate motivation for change. Several students in the group needed to learn basic social skills and acceptance for others. The group must become a social learning environment in which students can develop and practice effective interaction in a classroom style setting. Because the reading levels of the students are so diverse, any program developed for this group of children must offer individualized instruction if it is to succeed. Yet, because group social skills are so poor and diverse, these students desperately need the experience of working together in a positive, cohesive group. The program design must incorporate these needs as well.

Evaluate the needs of your group. What do your group members need? Remember to evaluate each participant as an individual, not just a member of a total group.

## Real-World Applications

### *Observational Extensions*

Once the group is formulated, get teachers or volunteers to help the students make name tags. Be creative. Don't just use the stickers that you write your name on; see the group intervention below for ideas. While the group members make name tags, sit back and observe group interaction in the group.

- How well do group members work together as a group?
- What problems do you see?
- Is everyone being included?
- Who are the domineering personalities in the group?
- What problems do you expect as the group starts?

### *Troubleshooting Checklists for Designing a New Group-Centered Program*

1. How much time will participants be expected to devote to your program? Will they have homework? Will students be taken out of class?
2. Where will your program be held?
3. How will transportation be handled?
4. Will participants be able to express grievances or complaints? Will they be able to complain to someone other than you?

5. Will participants be able to leave the program if they desire? Why or why not? How will you handle departures if they are allowed?

## A Ready-to-Use Group-Centered Intervention: "Sign-in, Please"

**Age level:** Second Grade through High School
**Learning Objective:** To initiate self awareness and group interaction and help group members identify feelings and experiences that they have in common.
**Counseling Objective:** To initiate interaction and to build group cohesion.
**Time needed:** 2 hours, depending on the size of the group.

*Tips for Using this Group-Centered Intervention*: Many name tag activities for groups have group members introduce their partner or other such approaches. The problem with group-wide introductions is that group members do not really get to know each other, or introductions turn into an "entertainment session" as group members try to surpass the preceding person with funny comments. Initiating interaction does not happen in a group-wide session where members take turns introducing each other. Instead, this group-centered intervention works from the strength of small groups. This exercise can also be used in a classroom setting with only one teacher or counselor.

*How to Expand into a Group-Centered Prevention Program*: This name tag group-centered intervention can be used as an introductory exercise that initiates interaction in a long-term or on-going program. Use the drawing or questions to help your group explore topics on a deeper level. For example, "look for someone who listed similar characteristics for a friend (You can also use totally opposite characteristics.). Work with this person today at the learning center workstations."

*Supplies needed*: 4×6 index cards, pencils, and colorful markers, crayons, or colored pencils

1. Have each person print their name neatly in the upper right hand corner of their card.

2. In the lower right-hand corner, have each participant write their favorite activity or hobby.

3. In the lower left-hand corner of the card, have participants describe their favorite time of the day.

4. In the upper left-hand corner, have participants write one or two words that describe characteristics they like about their best friend. Do not include any names, just characteristics, such as kind, considerate, helpful, honest.

5. In the center of the card, have participants draw a picture of the kind of person they perceive themselves to be. This is not a drawing of how you look physically, but a drawing of how you feel inside. Someone might feel like an electrical outlet

with too many plugs connected. Someone else might feel like a granule of salt in a salt shaker. Encourage students to let their imaginations soar. If students are not sure how they feel, then have them draw a picture of their confusion.

6. Then, on the back of the index card, have students write what they hope to achieve from this new group.

7. Allow about 10 minutes for group members to complete their name tags.

8. Then, count off into pairs. Have pairs explain their name tag to their partner. Keep the pace brisk. Allow about 10 minutes.

9. Next, have each pair join another pair to form a foursome. Have each person introduce his or her partner to the others. Allow about 20 minutes.

10. Have each foursome join another foursome and introduce again. Allow 40 minutes.

11. Reconvene as a total group. Do not sit around tables or in rows; use a circle of chairs. Allow everyone to tell about their pictures in the center of their name tags. Keep pace brisk. Allow about 40 minutes.

12. Close with an emphasis on factors that we have in common.

# Chapter 5
# Using Group Process as an Agent of Change

*She was a third grader reading at the first grade level. Her self-esteem was extremely high, and she did not feel that she needed help in reading. It soon became obvious that she compensated for her lack of skills by laughing at others or saying hurtful comments about other students who were struggling to read. Her battle plan: keep attention away from her problems by pointing out everyone else's problems. She made certain that she announced the problem in a very loud voice every time anyone made a mistake.*

*Teasing is not uncommon with students struggling to learn to read, and my usual approach is to announce, "We're a team; we work together; we absolutely never laugh at or make fun of anyone. We're here to help each other, so find a way that you can help someone today." My reminder worked for most of the group but not for her. She continued and I took her aside in the hallway and told her that she was not allowed to make fun of or laugh at other children at Camp Sharigan. She stopped for the remainder of the session, although she did not attend the next day. I worried that she might drop out as the program is strictly voluntary, but on the third day she returned. She almost laughed at the little boy working alongside her at the spelling station, but stopped before she did, and said instead, "Use the letter tiles; we'll spell the word together." Her behavior continued to improve. She learned to work with others instead of laughing at them. Not only did working in a supportive group structure help her to improve her own reading skills, but the group also helped her learn to work with others in a classroom setting.*

This third grader had developed a pattern of laughing at others to cover up her own lack of skills. Making fun of others had become a behavior pattern for the student. When she joined the group, she brought her previous behavior patterns with her. I stress a cohesive atmosphere in group programs and try to not enforce a long list of rules, but laughing at or making fun of others should never be tolerated in any group and definitely not in a group-centered prevention program striving to rebuild self-efficacy, but I also wanted to understand the third grader's needs. First, her teasing of others had to stop, and then I wanted to know why she felt so insecure and felt the need to attack others. I wanted to help her to change her behavior and develop new group skills in addition to improving her ability to read.

Clanton Harpine, *Group-Centered Prevention Programs for At-Risk Students*, DOI 10.1007/978-1-4419-7248-4_5, © Springer Science+Business Media, LLC 2011

## The Advantages of Using Groups

The major purpose of counseling and therapeutic interventions is to bring about change. Groups bring about as much if not more change than individual counseling (Hoag and Burlingame 1997) because it is easier to change in a group (everyone's working on a problem), easier to test and redevelop new ways of behaving in a safe group environment, and easier to reconstruct the classroom experience in a group program rather than in one-on-one tutoring or individual counseling; therefore, new skills learned are more easily transferred back to the classroom. A group also allows students to experience the real everyday problems of peer pressure, teasing, conformity, frustration, failure, and the need to belong in a safe, cohesive, supportive group.

Students can lose their feelings of failure in a cohesive group. Research shows that groups help participants change their behavior (Yalom and Leszcz 2005), especially in schools (Buhs et al. 2006). Groups are the logical avenue of change in school, but not all school groups lead to positive change. We must be careful to make sure that the groups we organize are positive and that they create strong, cohesive environments for constructive change.

## Using Group Process to Bring About Change

The majority of mental health services for children and youth take place in the school. The most common prevention interventions used in schools today are psychoeducational prevention programs.

*Psychoeducational group prevention programs.* Many prevention specialists use a psychoeducational format, and there is evidence supporting the effectiveness of psychoeducational prevention programs in school-based settings (Horne et al. 2007). Many professionals in the field warn that prevention programs should not become a lecture session disguised as a psychoeducational program. Merely grouping students together in a circle of chairs while you deliver a lecture on the dangers of drugs or the undesirability of bullying is not a psychoeducational prevention program. Adding role-playing to a lecture also does not meet psychoeducational standards. For a psychoeducational program to be effective, it must include group interaction (Conyne 2004).

Yet, prevention programs used in schools today do not always incorporate group interaction, and classroom lectures are all too common. Furthermore, groups through schools are not as effective as private clinical groups (Hoag and Burlingame 1997). This is cause for alarm when we remember that the majority of mental health services for children and adolescents are conducted through the schools, that groups are one of the best mediums of change, and that groups are frequently used in school-based mental health. A change is needed and we must increase the effectiveness of school-based counseling groups in schools and in the community. One answer might be a new approach to using groups in school-based settings.

*Group-centered prevention programs.* Group-centered prevention programs do not use the same group structure as a psychoeducational group program (Clanton Harpine 2008), and the *school-based mental health approach* uses only group-centered interventions and group-centered prevention programs. Group-centered prevention programs use hands-on activities and stress intrinsic motivation and group cohesion. Direct instruction or lecture is never included in a group-centered prevention program. While psychoeducational prevention programs stress imparting information, group-centered prevention programs stress rebuilding self-efficacy through skill building hands-on activities in a classroom-type environment. Individualized change is easier to accomplish in a group-centered program than with a psychoeducational program. Group interaction and group cohesion are built into every group-centered prevention program. Group-centered prevention programs use a positive group setting and stress interaction, focusing on cohesion as one of the necessary steps toward change.

Cohesive groups, based on a positive structure, form a supportive environment which contributes to mental wellness and the ability to adapt and cope with the real world (O'Brien Caughy et al. 2008), especially the world as experienced through a classroom. Students become more aware of how they learn in the classroom, how they interact with others in a group, and how others react to them. The goal of a group-centered prevention program is to change how children think about themselves and how they learn.

## Group Process and Group Dynamics are not the Same

When we talk about group counseling, we often see the terms "group dynamics" and "group process" used interchangeably, but these two terms describe different properties of the group. Group dynamics refers to the communication styles of participants in a group, the eagerness with which students participate in a group, the resistance, fear, anger, or avoidance that is displayed in a group, nonverbal behaviors within the group, or the expression of feelings (happy or sad); in other words, the dynamic differences that comprise the individuals who make up the group (Posthuma 2002). Group process refers to the patterns of interaction that occur between group members and the group culture that develops within the group. As with the student introduced at the beginning of the chapter, her communication style was to cover up her own fear of failure by verbally attacking others (group dynamics). When she was in a group setting, her interactions were aggressive and domineering, pointing out the mistakes and weaknesses of others. Such aggressiveness changed how the group functioned, what the group was able to accomplish, and how others in the group interacted with her (group process).

Group process is created through the techniques and interventions that you use in your group to generate interaction and cohesion. The dynamics of the group are the factors you have to work with based upon the members who comprise your group.

## Help! This is an Impossible Group

Sometimes you must change the dynamics of your group before you can conduct a successful program. As in the opening example, it may be only one group participant, and if that is the case, you can simply work with that individual, but often, it is a small group within the larger group. Such a small group can begin to form a group structure different from what you have planned, particularly if the small group is misbehaving or aggressive.

If you decide, after completing the group analysis in Step 4, that there is no way your group members can work together in a cohesive, cooperative group structure, then you may need to do some group work before you actually start your prevention program.

If the dynamics of your group will interfere with the success of your program, you may want to do some group restructuring before you start your actual prevention program. An example comes from a group of public school children with whom I used restructuring techniques. This group could represent any classroom at any grade level.

There was a cluster of four children in a group of 12 who exhibited constant behavior problems every week. Even though these four children did not comprise a majority of the group, they consumed a majority of my time. They also prevented positive group interaction and inhibited the development of a truly cohesive atmosphere because they were always in trouble. Their behavior exemplified a situation often found in a typical classroom.

*Restructure the group to implement change.* I divided the 12 children into three small groups and had them meet on different days for about 3 weeks. One small group was very shy, so I worked on building their confidence and teaching them how to take the initiative to interact in a group. The second group was very active (attention deficit hyperactivity disorder [ADHD]) and needed to work on control in the classroom. The third group was made up of the four students who were exhibiting behavior problems. With these four students, I would start a reading activity, and as soon as they would begin to misbehave, we stopped and talked about their behavior, not as a lecture but as a group: Why do you feel that you need to act that way in the group? How do you think it makes others feel? Would you like to change how you act in this group? How can we help you change? Often the group time was spent discussing behavior issues rather than working on the reading activity, but the results were tremendous.

*Identify and isolate problems.* By pulling the students away from the total group for 3 weeks, I was able to isolate the problem behavior, work on correcting it, and then return the students to the group of 12 and allow them to practice their new behaviors. Addressing the behavior problem directly outside of the total group allowed for direct attention to why students were misbehaving without destroying the overall group atmosphere. This kind of problem often occurs in the classroom because the teacher is so busy trying to control a handful of misbehaving students that shy students become overwhelmed; therefore, they crawl further into their shell and refuse to become involved in classroom activities. By instituting pull-out small groups, I did not overwhelm the students who were shy or inflict strict disciplinary control on students who needed to become more open and willing to interact.

*Use small groups to work on individual problems.* Small groups allowed me to work on separate problems and then bring the group back together to practice new behaviors. This strategy works well in a school setting where you can pull out small groups one at a time. When changes occur in a group setting, such changes are more easily transferred back to the classroom because students have had the opportunity to practice the new behaviors and skills in a classroom-like group.

*Use the group structure to help students change.* You do not simply pull four misbehaving students out of the classroom, work with them for 3 weeks, and then send them back to class. Group restructuring is a step-by-step process. Each small group was busy learning new behaviors. The group of 12 could then practice new interaction skills within a safe supportive group environment while they worked on reading skills before returning to the classroom. If I had just continued to work with the 12 students as a total group, I would not have been able to help the students change their individual behaviors. The shy students would have remained shy; the misbehaving students would have continued to misbehave. If the group had continued as a total group of 12, dominating behaviors from misbehaving students would have controlled the group experience. By structuring group process with each small group, I was able to work on group skills and then pull the group of 12 students back together to combine their new group skills with academic skills before returning the 12 students to the classroom. Structuring group process provided the opportunity for change, but small groups must return and work together as a total group, as the group of 12 did before returning to the classroom or to an ongoing prevention program.

*Groups become the step-by-step process of change.* If misbehaving students are pulled out as a small group and then reinserted back into the classroom, as is often done in school counseling situations, the change from small group to classroom is too great; therefore, failure results. Moving students from a small group of four to a group of 12 and then to the classroom allows students more opportunity to change and correct their behavior in a group setting. Before these students could learn academically, they had to learn to work with others in a group because a classroom is a group. They had to learn to accept and give positive feedback to others. They also had to learn to think about the needs of others. Academic learning and behavioral growth and well being do truly work hand-in-hand together. Such a group intervention mimics typical classroom behavior and therefore allows for stronger transference from the intervention group to the classroom setting.

The group becomes a learning laboratory where students can experiment with new interactive group behaviors. Group process becomes your instrument of change, both academically and psychologically. Change, lasting change which translates back to the classroom (Obiakor 2001), will be the determining factor upon which your program's success or failure is measured (Kulic et al. 2004). Therefore, we need to pay particular attention to how we build change into our program design.

## Developing Positive Group Process

It is the opportunity to interact with others in a group that enables students to learn to give and receive constructive feedback, to show care and concern for others, to learn new skills, and to display trust and acceptance and in turn experience trust and acceptance from others. Groups help students learn to cope with the give and take of the real world. The classroom is a group, and students must learn how to function effectively in a classroom group. Groups can model good or bad behavior. Modeling is stronger in groups, which is why your group program must generate positive role models and constructive modeling situations.

As you develop your program design, you must build constructive interaction, cohesion, acceptance, positive feedback, and a supportive group environment into the program design. Your program must incorporate the individual needs of each group participant. Group structure, the way in which you organize your group program, can teach students how to work together cooperatively in a classroom, but you must structure how you use group process in order to bring about change. Change must be carefully crafted. Effective group process does not happen automatically when you organize a group.

## Formative Evaluations

A step-by-step formative evaluation helps to ensure that a prevention program meets the needs of the children and adolescents for which that program has been designed. This is an essential step in the programming process and becomes a very vital instrument for developing evidence-based prevention programs.

A formative evaluation provides a stronger basis for program development and a replicable format. A formative evaluation is also an excellent way to adapt a program to the specific needs of a particular target group.

The purpose of a formative evaluation is to seek information helpful to the design or implementation of a program through observation(s) in real world settings. Formative evaluation is not a test of validity or measure of whether the program is successful or not; formative evaluation looks at the process and is conducted to improve an existing program and/or for the design of a new program. Formative evaluation aids program development by observing the process and spotlighting constructive suggestions for change (Royse et al. 2006).

As you select a group format for your program, you may want to conduct a formative evaluation as I did, and test two or three group formats to see which works best with your group. Do not be afraid to change or adapt your format to fit the needs of your group members. Remember, every group is different.

# Formative Evaluation: Part 1

I evaluated my program design from Step 3. Supported by research findings (National Reading 2000) and direct observational experiences with at-risk readers, I selected a hands-on format for my reading program. I knew that I wanted to emphasize group interaction and group cohesion. At the same time, I wanted skill-building activities that would help rebuild a positive sense of self-efficacy with at-risk readers. I wanted a portable group program which could be used with groups from a variety of different schools and in the community. At the same time, the program needed to be individualized to meet the very specific needs of at-risk children. Group process was the key.

Groups have been identified as the most effective way for teaching reading (National Reading 2000), but research does not specify a specific group approach. Schools subscribe to reading groups and one-on-one tutoring but research does not substantiate that either of these interventions work best for teaching reading. In 2001, when I started developing group interventions for at-risk readers, I made the mistake of trying to work within the school structure instead of creating a separate group structure. Let me illustrate the problems by describing the formative process with six different interventions.

*Site #1: Traditional age-level classrooms.* At the first site, my team and I worked with 30 first through sixth grade students from a low socioeconomic inner-city neighborhood, 3 hours a day for 5 days. One of the oldest sixth graders in the group was 18 years old and still reading at the first grade reading level. All of the children had been removed from the public school for behavior problems. We used four separate classrooms with seven to eight students in each class. The students were divided by age. At first, the program utilized reading circles, such as those often used in public school classrooms. The children's attention span was short and their frustration was high, and when they encountered a word that they did not know, they simply gave up, closed the book, and refused to try.

I introduced hands-on activities by mid-week. Puppets, storytelling, and reading and following directions to complete a simple craft project were among the methods. Such hands-on activities motivated children, who had absolutely no interest in reading anything, to read to make a simple craft project accompanying a story. The hands-on motivators helped, but the week-long session was still not as successful as I had hoped.

*Site #2: On-on-one and pair tutoring.* At the second site, I used an 11-week program with 30 first through third graders who attended an after school program at an inner-city community center. Half of the children worked one-on-one with tutors each week for an hour, the traditional public school pullout tutoring format. In the second group (pair tutoring), each tutor worked with two children at a time. All tutors used the same hands-on activities – puppets, pop-up books, and word games. Neither one-on-one or pair tutoring was successful. None of the students wanted to read or work on the hands-on activities. These were the same hands-on projects used at Site #1. In one-on-one and pair tutoring formats, the hands-on activities were less motivating than in the age-level small groups at Site #1. Outside of the group structure, at-risk readers simply were not interested in reading or working on hands-on activities.

*Site #3: Small group hands-on learning centers.* At the third site, I used a week-long, 3 hours a day format with learning centers and hands-on reading projects. Twenty-four first through sixth grade children from a low socioeconomic inner-city neighborhood came in the evening after school. The group was divided into four learning centers stationed around one large room. The children rotated in age-level groups from table to table at designated intervals. Each learning center had a speci-fied reading assignment. The students followed step-by-step directions to complete projects. A teenage helper was stationed at each learning center.

Learning centers allowed children to work in small groups. Hands-on projects proved to be excellent motivators. Two children even gave up their weekly bike riding time to come to the reading clinic every night. Hands-on learning centers motivated the children more than one-on-one pull-out tutoring or classroom reading circles, but we had trouble keeping the children moving smoothly from center to center. Some students became bored because they completed the task faster than others in their age group – a common classroom problem.

## Formative Evaluation: Part 2

The program was working, but my program design was not complete. I still had problems. I needed an easy and efficient way to move the children around the room and to increase interaction. I needed to make the groups more cohesive and strengthen skill-building. I did not want just a fun hands-on reading program. I wanted a program that would actually bring about change in mental health as well as reading; change that would transfer back to the classroom. To accomplish such change, I needed a program that would teach at-risk readers to read at grade level while rebuilding their self-efficacy and developing their group skills for interacting successfully in the classroom.

My program would have to enable children to work on social skills as well as reading skills. Interaction in a group setting can provide the best framework for personal growth and change (Yalom and Leszcz 2005), but can learning centers and group structure be combined? I worried that learning centers would constrict the development of group process and so I went out to test my ideas.

*Site #4: Stressing ability level rather than age.* I retested the hands-on learning centers with a new group, using *treasure hunt maps* (Clanton Harpine 2010a) with 30 children, first through third grade. The group included approximately equal numbers of first, second, and third graders from a very low socioeconomic struggling neighbor-hood school. The program used a 4-day, 2 hours a day format with ten learning centers.

I expanded the number of learning centers, shortened the time, and controlled age-level participation to see if these changes would enhance motivation.

Stories which stressed teamwork and cooperation were added to the program. The written instructions at each learning center reinforced sharing and working as a team.

Upon arriving, each child received a *treasure hunt map* which distributed the number of children equally around the room to the learning centers. Instead of having children move from learning center to learning center as a small group (as with Site #3); children moved at their own pace with the aid of their *treasure hunt map*. The maps helped children to move around the room independently and spend more time at learning centers where they needed the most help, thereby individualizing instruction.

The children rotated from learning center to learning center, using *treasure hunt maps* and selected their reading level through a series of *stepping stones* (Clanton Harpine 2010a). The children started at Step 1 and worked their way up as they were able. Grade level designations were not used. Through the use of *stepping stones*, everyone worked up to full potential. Even when the weather turned unseasonably pleasant for spring in the Midwest, all but two children voluntarily completed the entire week (Clanton Harpine 2005b).

One student arrived on the first day and announced that he was only staying for 5 minutes just to see what was happening, but he completed all 4 days and asked whether we would be returning the next week because he wanted to continue with the program. This same child was being retained in the same grade for failure in reading and an uncooperative classroom attitude.

Learning centers were successful where age-level reading groups and one-on-one tutoring had failed. *Treasure hunt maps* and individualized instruction through hands-on learning centers allowed children to work at their own pace. Observers noted that using equal numbers of first, second, and third graders yielded a reduction in competition. Children were less inclined to say, "my project is better than yours" with the combined ages, but the groups still had not achieved the level of group cohesion that I desired. Therefore, I tried again.

*Site #5: Adding a unifying summer camp theme.* I returned to the community center from Site #2 to see if our new hands-on learning center approach would make a difference with the children from the pair tutoring and one-on-one tutoring sessions who had refused hands-on motivators during tutoring. This time we used a full 1-week, 5-day, 2 hours a day reading clinic. The program was given a fun, summer camp-like atmosphere to tie the learning centers together under one theme. The program was named *Camp Sharigan,* where children come to share the love of reading. Sharigan is a friendly snake puppet used with the stories and puppet plays; he teaches about phonics and working together as a team. Play is the language of children (Landreth 2002) and through play the children learned to share and take turns.

The camp used painted cloth wall hangings to transform the gymnasium into a make-believe summer camp. There were painted forests, a waterfall, a rainbow, and a sunrise to welcome the children as they arrived. There were ten learning centers. Each learning center featured a different hands-on group activity. An inflated air mattress served as *Mount Reading* and worked on spelling words. A tent draped in flowers provided a place for children to write their own stories. A make-believe roaring paper camp fire provided a great place to sit and read a chapter book. A cloth fishing pond called *Lake Read* had four cloth fish with hidden pockets and new reading tasks each day. The *Rainbow Bridge* worked on puppets and the camp stop sign encouraged everyone to stop and read a book. At *Sharigan's Snake Pit*, the children practiced phonics. The camp library had long *grapevines* filled with sight words, and at the *Camp Cabins* children created their own pop-up book. The camp included a make-believe *poison ivy vine* that stretched around the room to capture *tricky words*. Puppets and puppet plays were also used to teach phonics each day. *Treasure hunt maps* and the *stepping stone* concepts were incorporated as part of the ongoing program design (Clanton Harpine 2010a).

The same children (from Site 2) took the same hands-on projects from the previous unsuccessful one-on-one tutoring sessions and worked for 5 days, 2 hours a day after school, completing every project. This was an inner-city site, and the children came from a school which had been identified as a failing school for 4 years in a row. In follow-up interviews, every participant in the reading clinic wanted to sign up and participate again (Clanton Harpine 2005a). One little boy who had refused to read during tutoring sessions and refused to read during classroom sessions with the teacher came an hour early to sit outside the door and wait for *Camp Sharigan* to start. Not only were the children motivated to work on reading, but their reading scores also improved following the 1-week *Camp Sharigan* program. The children showed definite improvement in oral passages, sight words, and spelling (Clanton Harpine 2005a). These were the same children who would not even bother to try to read in previous one-on-one or pair tutoring sessions. Yet one successful run with a program did not prove that this was a good program design. I took *Camp Sharigan* to another site.

*Site #6: More than just a reading program.* *Camp Sharigan* was taken to another after-school program in order to retest with children from the projects in a small southern town, with schools plagued by discipline problems. This group engaged in daily fights, even though the program directors were very strict about discipline. Fights would break out on the school bus, playground, and in the neighborhood. Children teased each other constantly. Would the teamwork and group structure that was emphasized through *Camp Sharigan* help to change behavior as well as reading?

Children were encouraged to help each other at the learning centers. Word games created a fun positive approach for mastering hard to learn irregular vowel sounds. Hard to spell words gave children an opportunity to help each other as they played the word games and exercised control over competitive urges. The children also worked together throughout the week, helping one another as they painted their puppet stage and prepared to present a puppet play. One little girl was heard to say, "You can't talk to me like that; don't you remember *Sharigan* said we have to work together?"

The *Camp Sharigan* group-centered structure was working. Reading and social skills were both improving (Clanton Harpine 2007a). *Camp Sharigan* was fun and the children came back day after day to participate. By experimenting with different group structures, I was able to find an approach that worked best with at-risk readers, but *Camp Sharigan* is not just a reading program. Reading is the intervention used to change behavior and strengthen mental wellness. Reading then becomes the medium through which one can enact this change. If I had simply chosen a traditional classroom approach, such as reading groups or one-on-one tutoring, I would have missed an opportunity to help at-risk children become motivated and engaged in learning to read and change their behavior.

## Using Formative Evaluations in Designing an Effective Group-Centered Program

Formative evaluation, testing and retesting at different sites, taught several lessons, such as combining first through third graders in the same reading program created a more cohesive group than when I separated children according to age. Children were not as concerned about comparing their project or the success of a fellow classmate when placed in a combined age group. Nothing in the previous research literature suggests combining first, second, and third grade at-risk children together in one group would help reduce the stigmatization of being a slow reader, but that is what happened, and it was only through formative evaluation that this was added to the program design.

Formative evaluation also helped to filter through reading activities that at-risk children did not find motivating and enabled me to develop a remedial reading program that at-risk children found truly interesting and exciting. The activities that the children selected as the most motivating were the puppet plays, a pop-up story book, word games, funny stories, hands-on story-craft projects, writing stories, and action stories. Therefore, formative evaluation is vital for the testing and retesting of prevention program ideas. Do not simply settle for the first sign of success. Select a small group and retest at the same site or test at different sites.

## Developing a Group-Centered Prevention Program

The *school-based mental health approach* uses only group-centered interventions which stress hands-on learning in a cohesive group environment. The outline presented in Step 5 is for building a group-centered prevention program. The step-by-step worksheet for Step 5 will help you develop your program ideas into an effective group-centered program.

## *Step 5: Building a Group Structure that Leads to Long Term Change*

How does your program enhance group process?

What do you do to encourage group interaction between all group members?

How do you combine skill-building and counseling into your group design?

How does your program reduce the stigmatization of failure?

Does your program bring about change?

Does your program combine the academic and counseling needs of the children successfully in one program?

# Using the Results from a Formative Evaluation

Using *Camp Sharigan* as my design example, I have answered each question in Step 5 in reference to my formative evaluations. I based my responses on the last two test sites. At this point in the process of developing a program, you may not be ready to field test your program, if so, that's fine, base your answers on expected outcomes. Then, when you are ready, test to see if your expectations held true.

## Step 5, Design Example

*Camp Sharigan's* program design consists of a hands-on reading camp which focuses on reading, writing, and spelling in a fun atmosphere of play. I created a fun, brightly colored make-believe reading camp filled with hands-on reading activities. I decided to use ten learning centers for *Camp Sharigan* because learning centers foster necessary skill-building in small groups and because they allow for more individualized instruction. Given the wide range of abilities in my groups, I need to always solicit volunteers to work with the program, but learning center program packets ensure accurate replication of the reading and social skills being taught in the program each time. I monitor progress throughout the week through *grapevine reading strips* which I use at the camp. Through a learning center-based, hands-on group program, students will receive: (1) total engagement in the learning process, (2) intrinsic motivation, (3) the skills to rebuild a positive self-efficacy about reading and their ability to learn, and (4) group counseling through positive group interaction and the therapeutic power of working together in a cohesive group. Skill-building through intrinsic hands-on learning centers, then, becomes an essential component of the *Camp Sharigan* program. Hands-on learning center activities enhance motivation, teach skills, and foster group cohesion (Clanton Harpine 2007b). I use such techniques as pop-up-books, puppets, and the concept of *capturing tricky words* throughout the reading camp to motivate children to want to learn.

Through repeated formative field testing, the most motivating and successful group approach proved to be hands-on learning centers set in a 1-week, 2-hours-a-day reading camp format, combining first, second, and third graders in one 30-person group. Hands-on learning centers created a fun-filled motivational environment that kept children returning day-after-day to work on remedial reading skills.

*Enhancing group process. Camp Sharigan* offers a positive environment where children can learn without fear of failure, grades, or judgment. The *Camp Sharigan* approach is group-centered because the program emphasizes working together as a group to help and support one another. *Camp Sharigan* encourages group cohesion by teaching the children to work in teams, overcoming competition and failure, and building successful group interactions. Group cohesiveness, interpersonal learning, and catharsis are the most significant group factors for change (Yalom and Leszcz 2005). *Camp Sharigan* also emphasizes skills through the hands-on learning centers: phonics, oral reading, sight word practice, writing stories, and spelling skill-building activities.

The hands-on learning centers keep motivation high all week. The emphasis on reading and following directions not only motivates but also improves comprehension. The children not only understand what they are reading, but are also able to make a simple craft project following the directions that they read.

*Encouraging interaction.* *Treasure hunt maps* keep the group moving and help group members interact on an individual level one-to-one. *Treasure hunt maps* and learning centers individualize instruction and allow children to work at their own pace. Action stories and puppet plays encourage teamwork and group problem solving. The program has a group-centered emphasis while still retaining the bonus of individualized learning.

*Skill-building and counseling techniques combined.* Puppet plays are used to teach phonics. Because they enjoy the puppet play, the children are motivated to work and solve the word problems that the puppet plays pose. Puppet plays also teach teamwork, cooperation, and turn taking. For example, the children work all week to make puppets and prepare a puppet play which challenges even the best of the readers in the group. They paint their puppet stage and help each other sound out hard words.

Individualizing instruction through *steps* instead of grade levels and by individualizing pacing through the use of a simple *treasure hunt map* charting their way around the room from learning center to learning center, all 30 children work together harmoniously. Placing a teenage/adult helper at each learning center allows for one-on-one assistance for those who need help at each learning center. Instruction is truly individualized.

*Reducing stigma of failure.* A technique called *stepping stones* (Clanton Harpine 2010a) is used with the *Camp Sharigan* program to provide individualized instruction without a grade level distinction. In that way, third grade students still reading at the first grade level will not feel stigmatized by age level designations. Everyone starts at Step 1 and works their way up toward Step 4.

*Change.* Creating a new, separate learning environment through *Camp Sharigan* brings about change, not only in learning, but also in behavior. By creating a new group and learning to work together in that group, children learn new rules for their behavior. *Camp Sharigan* is only a 10-hour, 1-week program, but an intense 1-week program can bring lasting change that is still evident 1 year later (Clanton Harpine and Reid 2009a). The children are eager to work on skill-building reading tasks for 2 hours after school and also eager to learn to work together as a cooperative, cohesive group in a classroom group structure (Clanton Harpine 2005a).

*Academic and counseling combined.* The emphasis on reading does not take away from the intrinsic appeal of the motivators. Children returned day after day, eager to work on reading after a full day at school. One little boy even cried when his mother arrived early and said he had to go home. About 10 minutes later, the little boy and his mother returned and she said, "I offered him candy, cookies, even TV time; he just wants to come back and be in the puppet play. What time are you finished?"

## Creating a New Program

Testing and retesting at six separate sites allowed me to create a program that truly worked in a real world setting with at-risk children. Not stopping at the first sign of success at Site 3 but continuing to develop and change the group format through observation and formative evaluation enabled me to develop a more comprehensive program. The resulting *Camp Sharigan* program provides a motivating environment in which children want to work day after day.

The troubleshooting checklists provided at the end of each chapter will help you evaluate your program design. Use observation and evaluation as developmental tools when creating a new program.

## Real-World Applications

### *Observational Extensions*

The examples given in this chapter show how important it is to observe what occurs in a group. If possible, videotape or bring in outside observers to evaluate your group programs. Then go over the tape and/or evaluations from your observation team and make a list of changes that you want to make to your program design. No one designs a perfect program the first time. Program design is a step-by-step process.

### *Troubleshooting Checklists for Designing a New Group-Centered Program*

1. How will improvement be measured in your program?
2. What will you do if participants do not show improvement?
3. Will participants be able to notice their improvement or will you have some way to show their improvement without the group becoming competitive?

## A Ready-to-Use Group-Centered Intervention: "Match the Sound"

**Age level:** Any age
**Learning Objective:** To help the student distinguish vowel sounds and match
  vowel sounds through a hands-on activity.
**Counseling Objective:** To strengthen group skills and enhance curative power of
  group process.
**Time needed:** 1 hour – can be repeated with new words

*Tips for using this group-centered intervention*: This group-centered intervention
works well with any age by simply adjusting the degree of difficulty to meet the
needs of the students. This is a great hands-on group intervention for students who
struggle with phonetic sounds. You can expand this intervention by substituting
new words and even new sentences. You may use words on flash cards or make
cards specifically for the game.

*How to expand into a group-centered prevention program*: You can also play the
game on multiple days. For example, you might start the game on Monday and tape
the words up on the wall. Play the game each day but not finish the game until
Friday. New words could be used each day and added to the words from the previous day. By taping the game up onto the wall, in a corner on the floor, or on a table,
you allow students to build on their knowledge each time and review what they
learned earlier.

*Supplies needed*: Stiff paper for words and sentence or word flash cards

1. Write a sentence on a stiff strip of paper. Write a sentence which uses several
   vowel sounds such as: The fluffy brown caterpillar will turn into a beautiful blue
   butterfly. Write words divided into syllables: The fluff.y brown cat.er.pil.lar.
2. Dividing words into syllables will make it easier for the children to play the
   game because the children will be matching new words to the vowel sound in
   each syllable.
3. Select flash cards or make flash cards from words that will correspond to your
   sentence. You want to make sure that some of the words on your flash cards can
   be matched to syllables on your sentence. For example, cards for the sentence
   from above might include such words as: cap, butler, eight, bill. Remember to
   match the vowels sounds, not the actual letters or the consonant sounds. Older
   students might match the first vowel sound in a multisyllable word. They are
   only matching the vowel sounds. The purpose is to help children focus on the
   vowel sounds.
4. You may also decide to include some words which cannot be matched. For
   example, the word *air* would not match in my sentence from Step 1.
5. When you are ready to start the game, make sure you explain to students that you
   are matching only the vowel sounds. Read over the sentence with the students.
   For young students, you may want to circle each vowel sound in your sentence
   so that they do not become confused and try to match to the consonant sound

which starts each syllable. Explain the difference between consonants and vowels.

6. For the first round of cards, start with some easy words which are an obvious match until the students understand the game. Then, make the game a bit more challenging in round two. Once everyone has mastered playing the game, then add some words that do not match along with those that do.

7. Do not give prizes or awards. Extrinsic rewards reduce actual learning that takes place. Let children play the game for the fun of learning something new. Let the game itself be the only reward.

8. If you are playing the game over several days or a week, tape each matched word above or below the syllable it matches in the sentence. If space allows, you might make a long string of words.

This game illustrates how the fun of working together in a group can help motivate students to want to learn. Learning really can be fun.

# Chapter 6
# Group Process and Motivation

*He was quiet but not shy. He greeted me with a smile every day as he arrived.*
*The school had labeled him as having attention deficit hyperactivity disorder*
*(ADHD). He wasn't the least bit hyperactive: never a behavior problem, very polite*
*and always wanting to follow directions, but he did have trouble staying focused*
*and on a task. As the teacher said, "he simply drifts off into his own little world."*
*I remember one day at Camp Sharigan when he plopped down in the middle of the*
*Rainbow Bridge and started reading. He read one book after another. Reading was*
*difficult for him; therefore, he didn't really like to read and rarely voluntarily chose*
*to read. It was wonderful to see him sit down in a pile of books and enjoy reading.*
*He came over to show me a book he had found. He was so excited as he explained*
*all about the story. I suggested that he take the book home with him that evening*
*and read the book to his little sister. He couldn't wait. When the session ended and*
*parents arrived, his little sister was with his mother. He hurried over to his little*
*sister and explained very proudly that he had found a new book and he was going*
*to read it to her on the way home. He went on to say, "You're going to love this*
*book; it's great. Wait till you're old enough to read."*

*Camp Sharigan* creates a motivational environment in which students find the
desire or choose to become motivated, but *Camp Sharigan* itself, cannot motivate
children. You cannot motivate another person. You can create a motivating environment, but you as a teacher, counselor, community leader, or parent cannot actually
motivate the student. True motivation must come from within. Motivation involves
the internal workings and processes which energize and direct our behavior (Reeve
et al. 2003), but the world around us often influences our actions. This is especially
true in the classroom because many teachers only use extrinsic motivators (prizes
or awards). Intrinsic and extrinsic motivation are not the same. Intrinsic motivation
is an internal desire. Extrinsic motivation is based on a reward (prize) or fear of
punishment. Intrinsic motivation enhances psychological well-being (Salovey et al.
2000). Extrinsic rewards may actually discourage students rather than offer encouragement because, once the reward is gone, so is the motivation (Thorkildsen 2002).
Extrinsic motivators (rewards, prizes, candy, food) do not lead to intrinsic motivation
or positive self-efficacy. Rewards or prizes are only substitutes for inner motivation
that is lacking. At first, extrinsic motivators seem to work, but actually, extrinsic

Clanton Harpine, *Group-Centered Prevention Programs for At-Risk Students*,
DOI 10.1007/978-1-4419-7248-4_6, © Springer Science+Business Media, LLC 2011

motivators are merely a form of regulation; they are methods for seeking compliance which often backfire because once the extrinsic motivator is removed, children are sometimes less interested in learning than before you used the extrinsic motivator (Lepper and Greene 1975).

All students have three basic needs in the classroom: (1) competence, having specific skills, knowledge, or ability; (2) autonomy, being self-determining or having a feeling of control; and (3) relatedness, being able to demonstrate a connection between basic skills and performing a skill successfully in a classroom of one's peers (Deci and Ryan 1985). It is the fulfillment of these needs that leads to intrinsic motivation (Urdan and Turner 2005). Perceived ability (self-efficacy) to control or regulate the learning environment leads to academic success (Zimmerman et al. 2005). Therefore, there is a definite relationship between self-efficacy, intrinsic motivation, and achievement. Programs that reduce academic failure and increase academic competence also reduce depressive symptoms and increase a student's perception of control (Rudolph et al. 2001).

## Intrinsic Motivation Helps Students Cope with Unexpected Situations in the Classroom

We are an inherently active species. We build with our hands, play games, read action stories, solve puzzles; in short, we find activities that interest us and provide enjoyment. The environment in which we live (home, community, and world around us) is constantly changing. We adapt, grow, and change each and every day as we react to new experiences, and we have individual interests. We are stimulated or not stimulated, make adjustments or fail to adjust. We develop skills, seek challenges, and try new adventures and tasks. The manner in which we approach and tackle these changes is controlled by the internal controls which regulate our behavior and actions. These internal controls are regulated by intrinsic (internal) needs or extrinsic influences from the environment.

If a student feels free to choose to engage in an activity, then the more satisfied and committed the student feels to continuing and completing that activity to the best of their ability. If a student feels pressured or forced, then the choice becomes frustrating and interferes with the need to seek enjoyable, interesting activities. The way in which the classroom or group environment supports or frustrates this intrinsic need will determine the student's motivation, productivity, and well-being (Deci et al. 1995; Deci and Ryan 1985).

When students feel controlled or trapped, they do not feel engaged in interesting and enjoyable activities. Over time, students perceive that they do or do not have the skills to interact with their environment and control the effect that the classroom has on their life. The ability to adapt and cope in a positive manner to one's environment is essential for mental health, because a sense of failure or "giving-up" can develop into a state of learned helplessness and eventually into depression (Seligman 1990). Students are bombarded with unexpected problems in the classroom every day. The student's ability to positively cope with unexpected situations leads to healthy development and wellness.

## Intrinsic Motivation Helps Students Achieve Psychological Wellness

Intrinsic motivation is part of the counseling technique that we wish to incorporate into our program design in order to enhance mental health and well-being. This chapter shows how to develop intrinsic motivators to add to a program design. It is not enough to simply think of a creative program idea. To develop an effective group-centered prevention program, we must ensure that the program design meets the students' needs. All students need intrinsic motivation.

## Creating an Intrinsic Learning Environment

The *school-based mental health approach* does not use extrinsic awards or prizes but instead stresses incorporating six intrinsic motivators into the learning environment of the program: a positive self-efficacy, efficacy expectations (exercising control), outcome expectations (persistence), choice (freedom to choose), competence-affirming feedback (experiencing progress and success), and being self-directed (commitment). These six intrinsic motivators are essential for change and wellness in school-based mental health (Ryan and Deci 2000). They are also essential for the development of an effective group-centered prevention program. Let us look at each of these concepts individually. We will then discuss how to build these concepts into a program design.

*Intrinsic Motivator #1: A positive self-efficacy.* Self-efficacy is not only instrumental in academic improvement, but it is also motivating. Students need to see improvement before they will begin to change their self-image and believe that they can learn. When designing an effective school-based prevention program we must create an environment which will lead to positive self-efficacy for all students.

Skill-building activities increase the student's confidence and ability by increasing control and also by increasing the connectivity or organization of fibers within the brain (Keller and Just 2009; Meyler et al. 2008). Classroom prizes and rewards, such as pizza or candy, do not bring about such changes in the brain and may actually discourage a student's natural intrinsic desire to learn (Fawson and Moore 1999). With mandated testing, students stay focused on producing correct answers instead of discovering the joy of learning new information or solving a problem (Condry and Chambers 1978). Extrinsic rewards (such as candy and pizza) only motivate temporarily, if at all, and bribes and prizes do not lead to self-efficacy. Self-efficacy, then, is the catalyst for change that we must build into school-based interventions. Positive self-efficacy through improved skills must be built into every hands-on activity.

*Intrinsic Motivator #2: Efficacy expectations (exercising control).* Allowing students to exercise control does not mean choosing or not choosing to learn. Exercising control means choosing alternative pathways to how one learns. Intrinsic motivation occurs when the student finds interesting and enjoyable activities which encourage the student to master and complete optimal challenges (Deci and Ryan 1985). When students engage in school work and feel competent and able to complete the task, then the student is feeling intrinsically motivated or experiencing self-determination (control). Students' desire to exercise control is determined by their belief or perception (self-efficacy) that they have the power to control the situation or produce the desired classroom results on a test or activity. Perceived control over one's environment is essential for mental health and well-being (Bandara 1986).

When the student's skills are not capable of meeting the challenges of the classroom, the student feels overwhelmed, worried, or threatened. When the student's skills outweigh the task, the student is bored because there is no challenge. Being overchallenged (threatened) or underchallenged can cause psychological problems. At the same time, low challenge for low-skilled students creates apathy or sometimes even anger and aggression as demonstrated by our teenager from Chapter 2. "I wish my middle school teachers could see me now," she said as she finished reading a first grade level book. "They gave me coloring pages every day in middle school because they said I couldn't read and there was no way to teach me."

We must be careful not to underchallenge or overchallenge students. As we develop a program design, we must incorporate optimal challenge for all students without giving up or being threatening and overly controlling with those who struggle. Schools sometimes try to motivate students by pushing too hard, too fast, such as our student in Chapter 2 who tested at the pre-primer level (below first grade) and went from coloring pages in middle school to being taught second grade material her freshman year in high school as the school said, "to challenge her." Such tactics never work, because when the challenge is beyond the skill level of the student the student will fail. Students usually experience the most academic success and pleasure from moderate challenges (Schunk and Pajares 2005), but to meet the challenges of the classroom, at-risk students must be given the skills needed to complete the work assigned. Without skill-building, even moderate challenges will prove unsuccessful.

At *Camp Sharigan*, children work for 2 hours after school on reading, spelling, and writing skills. Even though some schools assign students to the program because of failing grades, the children must ultimately make the decision to stay in the program. It is a voluntary program, therefore, students must choose to come each day after school and work on classroom tasks rather than go home and watch television or go outside and play. The children choose the level of difficulty or challenge through the *step system* used. They are able to complete the challenges or steps because of the skills being taught at each learning center.

*Intrinsic Motivator #3: Outcome expectations (persistence).* To succeed, students must expect success in the classroom. For students to expect that they will succeed, classroom activities or after school programs must generate motivation with high effort and strong persistence.

Schools often use grades as motivators, but this can actually discourage students. An example comes from a school district seeking to comply with mandated testing. In an effort to raise test scores, the school district offered a midsemester district exam. To motivate the students, the school district ordered that the exam count for

10% of the student's overall grade (a common practice in many schools). Over half of the students failed the exam. In order to not discourage students from continuing to work for the remainder of the semester, the school district put a cap on failing scores and determined that all failing grades would be rounded up to a numerical grade of at least 60. Grades above 60 were not changed. This led one student to state, "Why did I bother to study? I could have taken the 60 and been as well off." Neither the grades nor the exam were intrinsically motivating. When the grade reward did not seem profitable, the student's conclusion was, why bother. This is the problem with extrinsic motivators (grades); they work only as long as the reward is forthcoming and deemed desirable.

In contrast, at the *Camp Sharigan* reading clinic, a little boy was working at the *grapevine station*. The children had been asked to read until they captured five *tricky words*. The little boy had captured four words but seemed a bit frustrated. Wanting to keep his experience positive, I said, "four's plenty; go ahead and put your words up on the *poison ivy vine*. Then, go see what's at the next station." He looked at me; looked back at the paper *grapevine,* and said, "I can find one more." The little boy continued reading until he found another word that he did not know. Capturing a word at *Camp Sharigan* means finding a word that you do not know or cannot read and then following four steps to learn the new *tricky word*. The little boy could have stopped and saved himself extra work, but instead, he chose to continue. Intrinsic motivation includes the freedom to choose to learn, to try.

*Intrinsic Motivator #4: Choice (freedom to choose).* Intrinsic motivation is essential for success in school (Sternberg 2005). Students' perception of their ability to succeed or fail in the classroom often determines the actual outcome displayed on a student's report card. For children to succeed, they must be motivated to learn (Baker et al. 2000). To feel motivated, children must experience self-determination (Deci and Ryan 1985). Self-determination is the freedom to choose to learn rather than being forced to do so (Deci et al. 1995). The child learns for the pleasure of learning or the desire to acquire knowledge. A child's motivation to learn without the promise of external rewards or fear of punishment encourages self-determination (Ryan and Deci 2000).

At one *Camp Sharigan* site, a student was reluctant to attend the after school program. The camp was being used for the lowest scoring children or those who had been identified as failing for that particular grading period. At this community-based site, the students who were not selected to participate in *Camp Sharigan* went out to play on the playground for 2 hours while the *Camp Sharigan* children worked. It was understandable that the young man might have chosen to play rather than work on reading. The teacher attempted to coax the young man into participating in the *Camp Sharigan* program by offering candy as a reward if the young man would at least try. The young man reluctantly joined the group. He stayed for the entire 2-hour session and returned each day for the remainder of the week. He never received the candy promised him by the teacher, nor did he even remember to ask for it. He also never asked if he could leave and go join the group playing on the playground. Extrinsic, candy bribes are not true motivators. They do not last and they will not bring about a change in self-efficacy. Intrinsic motivators help students get excited about learning.

In order to build positive self-efficacy into group-centered prevention programs, students must be encouraged to want to learn rather than to go outside and play.

*Intrinsic Motivator #5: Competence-affirming feedback (experiencing progress and success).* Children have a natural desire to succeed in the classroom and to experience success. To succeed and feel successful is a basic psychological need, but children need different types of teaching strategies. No two children are the same and no two children learn in the same way. We cannot continue to use the same teaching method for all children. We must offer a variety of teaching methods in order to fit the learning styles of all children. If we continue to teach using only one approach, as in our earlier example of the blue ribbon school (in Chapter 2) which taught solely through worksheets, we will continue creating mental health problems in the classroom. Classroom teaching methods can and do contribute to the number of school-based mental health problems identified every year.

When we teach with only one method, we teach children that they are a failure simply because they were unsuccessful in learning using that one method. Perceptions of failure are not motivating. Perceptions of competence are motivating; therefore, it is important to build success steps into the program design.

An example comes from a 6-year-old child assigned to one-on-one tutoring. After a few weeks, the tutor reported that the child would not be able to learn to read. The tutor went on to say that "the child's ADHD. He will never learn to read in a classroom. I know what the program says, but I am going to use a more traditional approach with him."

Unfortunately, the "more traditional approach" used methods which had already failed with the student in the public school classroom, which is why he was placed in one-on-one tutoring. The child was later placed in my after school program and he was not actually diagnosed with ADHD. The little boy was very smart and had a developmentally normal attention span. Even though his listening and processing skills were excellent, he responded better to hands-on activities. His biggest problem was that he was an active, normal six-year-old boy. He was accustomed to playing computer games and watching television at home. Computer games and a heavy reliance on television often make it hard for young children to sit quietly and learn when they first go to school. The computer-age child is conditioned for active, quickly changing stimuli. Books do not flip from one scene to another. It sometimes takes a while to retrain children away from a heavy diet of computer games and television. Hands-on techniques engage the child in a new learning approach. Hands-on skill training projects helped the child learn to focus on an assigned task and choose to complete that task instead of giving up.

*Intrinsic Motivator #6: Being self-directed (commitment).* In order to encourage children to become self directed, children must choose to learn. Intrinsic motivation allows children the freedom to choose. Research indicates that at-risk students often are not able to work well or achieve their full potential in a traditional classroom structure (Morris et al. 1990). The classroom structure can become an important ingredient in creating an intrinsically motivating environment but simply being creative is not enough. Creative ideas will not necessarily bring about academic success.

# How to Use the Six Motivators in Your Program Design

Each of the hands-on projects at *Camp Sharigan* incorporates these six motivators. As an example, the pop-up book, one of the most popular hands-on projects, integrated the six intrinsic motivators (1) by being positive, there were no right or wrong answers and no competition; (2) by allowing control, by encouraging children to chose how many pages to put in their book rather than having the teacher assign a set number, each page displayed a pop-up, therefore, the project could be easily adapted to varying skill levels without displaying an incomplete project; (3) by emphasizing persistence, the excitement and fun nature of making a paper pop-up book encouraged children to continue working on the project rather that giving up when the project became difficult; the children were highly motivated to finish their pop-up book, yet to finish, each child had to read, follow directions, and write a story; (4) the children could choose how to decorate their books, how many pages to add, and which story they wanted to write; (5) by emphasizing success, reading and following directions showed the children that they could read, comprehend, and make a project based upon what they read; and (6) by stressing commitment, the project encouraged children to read more difficult material, to not give up but rather to complete a project, as well as stressing comprehension. The pop-up book was a week-long challenging motivator that allowed each child to work at their own individual ability level.

An example of the intrinsic motivating power of the pop-up book project comes from an inner-city *Camp Sharigan* site. Many of the children lived in the floodplain of a river. It so happened that we experienced several hard days of rain during *Camp Sharigan*. Thursday evening the river flooded; the children and their families had to be evacuated from their homes. Many of the children spent the night under a tarp in the back of a pickup truck, and by Friday morning I did not expect strong attendance. All but two of the 30 children returned insisting that they wanted to finish their pop-up books. Several of the children were sick from being out in the rain all night, but they were standing, waiting quietly when the doors opened. The two children who did not return were both too sick to attend.

Go back and review your worksheets for Steps 1–5. Then look at the worksheet for Step 6. Think how you can incorporate intrinsic motivation into every facet of your program design. A creative idea does not guarantee intrinsic motivation. You must build intrinsic motivation into every aspect of your program.

## *Step 6: Building Intrinsic Motivators into Your Program Design*

### Describe Your Program Design

How can you build positive self-efficacy (motivator #1) into your program design?

How will you help students exercise control (motivator #2) and increase their positive efficacy expectations?

How will you measure success (motivator #3) and show students that they are improving? What outcome measures will you use? How will you keep these outcome measures from being interpreted negatively by students?

How will you incorporate a feeling of choice (motivator #4) into your program?

How will you measure effort and persistence?

How will the students experience progress and improvement (motivator #5), even beyond your testing or outcome measures? How will you challenge students? What precautions will you use to make sure challenges do not become negative avenues of defeat?

How will you help students become self-directed (motivator #6)?

How will you know that your intrinsic motivators are working?

**Step 6: Design Example**

The design for *Camp Sharigan* emphasizes phonics, spelling, sight words, oral reading passages, comprehension, and writing to increase the skill building necessary for the students to have a positive sense of self-efficacy. Combining first, second, and third graders into the same *Camp Sharigan* reading clinic also removed the stigma of age level appropriateness because there were so many different ages completing so many different activities that even the most competitive children soon lost count of who was doing what. The unique nature of making a pop-up book gave each child a sense of pride and accomplishment. The hands-on motivators and story craft projects became hands-on teaching tools that stressed the six intrinsic motivators outlined by the *school-based mental health approach*.

*Positive Self-efficacy.* At *Camp Sharigan*, words are never missed or incorrect, they are *captured*. The children go around hunting for tricky words to capture; each

word captured is added to a new word list strung around the room, called the *poison
ivy vine*. Children use a *4-step method* to learn these new words: (1) sound out the
words and use each word in a sentence, (2) tell the children the word's meaning, (3)
spell the word out aloud together, and then (4) have the children write the words
they *captured* on a poison ivy leaf and place the leaf on the poison ivy vine around
the room (Clanton Harpine 2010a). The children cheer at the end of the week when
they count how many new words they have captured. This simple word reversal
game makes learning new words fun. For example, an original game using the
camp theme, called *Grapevine,* features a long, curled piece of paper taped to a
table at the *camp library* learning center. The children uncurl the paper grapevines
and attempt to read as far as they can. They stop when they have captured five new
words. They take these five new words, use the *four-step method* (Clanton Harpine
2010a), and then place their captured words on the paper *poison ivy vine* encircling
the room. Each day children return to read a little bit further on the *grapevine*.
Often, children go back to test their skill at the *grapevine* even when not assigned
to do so. There is no failure, competition, or grading involved; children simply
enjoy the challenge of self-improvement. Such a game helps children see immediate
improvement. When children see themselves as making improvement, they then
want to try harder to make even more accomplishments. Such accomplishments
help to build positive self-efficacy because students see themselves as able to complete the *grapevine* task.

*Efficacy Expectations.* The children read as well as write stories at *Camp Sharigan*.
Sometimes they write an ending for a story; other times they write their own ver-
sions of a story. On the last day, for the parents' program, children line up at the
microphone to read their stories. The fun nature of *Camp Sharigan* motivates the
children to tackle harder reading and writing tasks. If you ask children to write a
story, many children will say they simply do not know what to write and sit for
hours not writing. If you give children an assignment, such as write three wishes,
most at-risk children will sit and say that they do not know what to wish for and
therefore end up writing nothing. In contrast, if you read a fun action story to children and stop right when something is about to happen, then children eagerly want
to write and tell what they think will happen next. I use this technique throughout
*Camp Sharigan*. I will start a session with a story or have a short story waiting at a
learning center station for the children to read. I will stop right at the climax and
say, "you're the author; tell what happens next."

*Outcome Expectations.* At *Camp Sharigan*, children achieve a desirable outcome by
reading and following directions; therefore, their outcome expectations rise with each
effort. There are no prizes or awards. Everyone works for the fun of working together
to accomplish something that they enjoy. *Camp Sharigan* maintains a fast pace, providing a constant stream of new hands-on projects and action stories so that the
children always find a surprise at each learning center. Learning centers change each
day. There are both 1-day projects which are quick and easy to finish, and week-long
projects which take the entire week to complete. The short-term, easy projects provide short immediate motivation, and the week-long projects provide ongoing

motivation for the week. Something new and hands-on is waiting for the children each day at *Camp Sharigan*. *Stepping Stones* also allow children to see daily success; therefore, children begin to expect success, as they experience success, children are more inclined to work a challenge step or to tackle more difficult material. Instead of worrying about failure or expecting to fail, children expect and experience success, such a feeling of success is motivating. Success is a strong motivator, but merely learning new words will not change a student's efficacy expectations about reading. The hands-on learning center must teach the necessary reading skills as well.

*Choice.* Pop-up books provide an excellent challenge because children can decide how many pages they want to include in their book, the number of decorations and pop-ups per page, and the story that their pop-up book will tell. To cut, fold, and work the paper into shapes that will pop up takes patience and control, and children select the level of difficulty and challenge that they wish to attempt. Each child, regardless of age, can write their own story and make a pop-up book. The challenge of writing a longer story and adding more intricate pop-up features encourages children to work up to their ability level.

*Competence-Affirming Feedback.* *Camp Sharigan* utilizes a technique called *stepping stones*. Everyone starts at Step 1 and progresses upward each day. It also uses *grapevine reading strips* which are nothing more than *vowel clustered* sight word lists presented in a fun, hands-on manner but which allow children to see themselves improving each day as they move further up the grapevine. Both techniques are noncompetitive and individually paced. Yet children get excited to see their improvement each day. Such competence building strategies only work if you also incorporate skills training which allows the children to make improvement. The fast hands-on pace of *Camp Sharigan* keeps children excited about learning and choosing to come back day-after-day.

*Self-Determination.* Children will decide to read or not read determined by how they perceive reading as necessary to maintain their self-image. A puppet play encourages children to challenge themselves to attempt more difficult tasks than they might normally be willing to perceive themselves capable of completing. The puppet play included at the end of Chapter 9 is a perfect example. The puppet play uses pollution terms which most of us will have to look up in the dictionary to pronounce. This becomes a fun way to help older students use the dictionary and challenge themselves to tackle harder material. At one site where the children presented this puppet play, a young man was misbehaving until I announced that I was seeking readers for our presentation of the play. He wanted to read and I assigned him a role; with a dictionary in one hand and his script in the other, he then began working hard to learn his part instead of misbehaving and getting into trouble.

*Evidence That Motivation Is Working.* One third grader who participated in the *Camp Sharigan* program enjoyed the program and stayed the entire week but was reluctant to challenge himself to reach his full potential. The young man was reading at grade level but actually capable of doing much better. On the first day of *Camp Sharigan*, the third grader went from station to station completing his work but never attempting to work any of the challenge steps. Challenge steps are used throughout *Camp Sharigan* to encourage children to try new material. By the second day, the third grader saw other children working the challenge steps and began to do the same. By the end of the week, the third grader had moved up a grade level in oral reading, sight words, and spelling, and he wanted to know if there was another challenge step or maybe a book that he could take home and work on. Intrinsic motivators instilled a desire for this young man to challenge himself beyond his comfort zone.

## Intrinsic Motivation is Essential for an Effective Group-Centered Prevention Program

No matter what the subject or set of skills you select to teach in your program: math, reading, history, science, public speaking, a sport, or even teaching someone to play a musical instrument; your program will not be successful nor will your students be truly motivated until participants begin to see improvement or feel a degree of competence in the skills you are teaching. Competence generates positive self-efficacy which determines the amount of effort put forth by the student and the persistence the student will exhibit (how long the student will continue to work) on a particular task without giving up. Therefore, you must build steps of intrinsic improvement into your program design.

## Real-World Applications

### Observational Extensions

Observe a group that uses typical extrinsic motivators such as awards, candy, or prizes. If possible, follow up by observing the same group using only intrinsic motivators. If you cannot observe the same group, observe at least a group that uses only intrinsic motivators.

- What is different about the groups?
- How do students react differently to the different motivators?
- How would you change the group from using extrinsic motivators to intrinsic?

### Troubleshooting Checklists for Designing a New Group-Centered Program

1. When you use extrinsic motivators, there is always a hidden motivational cost (not financial). Check your program design. Are you using intrinsic or extrinsic motivators? Can you convert all extrinsic motivators to intrinsic?

2.  Are you using rewards, punishment, reprimands, or extrinsic incentives? How can you change these to be intrinsic?

## A Ready-to-Use Group-Centered Intervention: "A Simple Pop-Up Book"

**Age level:**  Any age
**Learning Objective:**  To motivate students to write grammatically correct stories.
**Counseling Objective:**  To generate intrinsic motivation through a hands-on project.
**Time needed:**  1 hour

*Tips for Using this Group-Centered Intervention*:  This is a basic outline for a pop-up book. This pop-up house can involve simple crayon decorations for young children or elaborate windows and shutters with teens.

*How to Expand into a Group-Centered Prevention Program*:  You can also take this basic pop-up design and create a variety of pop-up structures. For example, at *Camp Sharigan* participants make the basic pop-up house, then add two additional pop-up pages for living room furniture and a bedroom. The students work on their pop-up house for 5 days. At *Sharigan's World Pollution Conference*, participants create a multilayered forest using the same basic pop-up concept. With the *Reading Orienteering Club*, participants create an ocean scene for *Ollie Octopus*. They spend 2 months creating the pop-up ocean scene.

This basic pop-up house activity can be used to initiate story writing and help students create their own book. Only the basic process of creating a pop-up house for this group-centered invention is described here. You may use this intrinsic motivator with whatever project you desire. Creating an entire book is a longer process, too lengthy to include in this chapter, but described in full in the week-long *Camp Sharigan* program.

*Supplies needed*:  construction paper – two sheets per student (one sheet should be green for the grass, and for the second sheet, have students select a color for their house), scissors, pencils, a ruler, glue sticks (use only glue sticks – no liquid glue), crayons or markers.

1.  Have students select a color of construction paper to use in making a pop-up house. Keep green construction paper set aside to use later for the grass.
2.  Fold construction paper selected for the house in half, as if you are making a book. Place the paper flat on the desk as if it were a book. On the open edge, measure down 4 in. from the top open edge. Draw a line from the 4-in. mark to the top centerfold of the paper. Cut along this line to form the roof of the house.
3.  Again, place paper flat on desk, as you would a book, this time on the bottom edge (The roof will be the top; the bottom edge will be opposite from the roof.) on the folded edge side, measure up the fold 1 in. Draw a 1½-in. line from the

1-in. mark on the fold to the bottom open edge of the paper. Cut the small triangle formed by this line.

4. Open your house and fold the flaps formed at the bottom when you cut the small triangle. Fold these flaps to the inside of your folded paper.

5. Open the house and lay it flat on the desk. Decorate the house. Flaps should be folded to the nondecorated side.

6. Take the sheet of green construction paper and fold it in half, like a book. Open the green construction paper and place it flat on the desk, open like a book.

7. Place the decorated house on the green sheet of paper. Put glue ONLY on the folded flaps (use only glue sticks).

8. Place the center fold of the house (that is where you cut the small triangle) on the center fold of the green paper. Place it in the middle of the green page. Press down the flaps to glue the house in place.

9. Open and close the green paper to make sure the house pops up before the glue sets. The house should pop up on its own when you open the green page. If not, return to Step #8 and reposition the house before the glue has a chance to dry.

10. Once the house is positioned correctly, leave the green paper open until the glue is completely dry.

11. You may use this pop-up house as a card, as a cover for a story, or as part of a book.

12. Students may write a story about the house they have made and the family who lives there. If you are using this intervention with children/teens who are experiencing trouble at home, you may have participants make their houses or apartments and have students write a story about something that happened at their house. I once wrote a story called *Problem City*. Each house, each family in *Problem City* was plagued with problems of all kinds. Students then wrote a story about their house and what would happen if their family moved to *Problem City*.

# Chapter 7
# The Role of Interaction in a Group

*She was listed as a third grader who had already been retained one year and was now being socially promoted in the face of reading failure. Her fall report card had listed another failing grade in reading. Her test scores showed that she was barely able to read at the first grade level. The school had diagnosed her with attention deficit hyperactivity disorder (ADHD) and she was receiving medication for it. Her mother stated that she wanted to take her daughter off medication because it wasn't helping, and enrolled her in my after school program asking, "Can you help her?"*

*The third grader had trouble staying focused on a task, following instructions, and completing assignments. She was impulsive, spoke very loudly, and displayed an obvious lack of control in the classroom. As a teacher said, "Not the sort of student for your freewheeling Camp Sharigan program." As it turned out, it was a perfect program for the student. Being a member of a cohesive group with hands-on motivational projects, especially the pop-up book, challenged the young student to work hard to control her ADHD behavior and finish her work. She was actually one of the first in the group to write her story for her pop-up book. She continued into the Reading Orienteering Club, a year-long follow-up tutoring program, and six months later was reading at the second grade level. Hands-on, intrinsically motivating group interaction had turned this student from failure to success.*

Just as it is not possible to not communicate because the mere act of not saying anything communicates your reluctance or lack of participation to others, it is also impossible to not interact. Interaction is the process of influencing one another. If I walk into a group and engage you in conversation, I am interacting with you. If I walk into a room, stand against the wall, and simply watch other group members, I am still interacting, but the interaction may not be positive or supportive for the group. If, however, I walk in and announce the direction the group will take and the rules by which the group will function, then, yes, I am interacting; I am also dominating and controlling the group and my dominance will stifle and control the interactions of others.

Group interaction is the way in which group members work together. Do they talk to one another? Are they helpful? Do they tease or act negatively toward certain group members? Is everyone included?

Clanton Harpine, *Group-Centered Prevention Programs for At-Risk Students*, DOI 10.1007/978-1-4419-7248-4_7, © Springer Science+Business Media, LLC 2011

For a group-centered prevention program to be successful, interaction must not be just between leader and participants. There must also be free-flowing, constructive interaction between all group members. That kind of interaction is not easy to attain.

Group interaction can be positive or negative. Interaction can support your program design and purposes or interaction can destroy your group. Effective interaction will not happen automatically; you must design positive interaction into your program. Positive interaction is a skill that needs to be taught to group members.

## Building Interaction into Your Group Design

We open the door to successful interaction through the way in which we have group members work together. Interaction begins the instant participants arrive. What is the first thing group members will see? What is the first thing they will do? For interaction to be effective, you need to structure the group's interaction from start to finish.

Structuring is not the same as controlling. You do not want to be a dictator or to stifle the group. Group members need to explore and feel free to interact together, but you want the group's interaction to be positive and to contribute to the group's development. Therefore, you must build positive group interaction into your program design.

There is a major difference between group-centered prevention programs, psychoeducational groups, and group psychotherapy. Psychoeducational groups use structure but emphasize the imparting of information and, often, the practicing of new behaviors. Group psychotherapy often deemphasizes structure and instead allows the group structure to grow out of the group and the interactions between group members. Group-centered interventions used in the *school-based mental health approach* establish a structure for the group, using group interaction to bring about the desired change. Cohesion and group process become the therapeutic factors; the rebuilding of self-efficacy through intrinsic motivation and skill-building interventions becomes the change transferred back to the classroom. Effective group-centered prevention programs must incorporate positive, supportive group interaction.

## A Strong Introduction is Essential to Positive Group Interaction

All group interaction is governed by rules. These rules may be explicit (formally announced or written) or implicit (not stated or written). Rules may be culturally based, applicable only to certain settings, or limited to certain kinds of groups.

Many people believe that when they start a new group they must explain the rules before they get started. Such rule sessions stifle interaction and group process. Instead of reading off a long list of rules, build the rules into how your group interacts. Allow the structure you create to define the rules. Start with interaction, not an explanation or long list of rules.

Everything you do adds to or detracts from group interaction. Think about what the first thing group members will do when they join your group session. Will students be sitting in chairs, on the floor, or standing? Will the students sit and listen to you talk or dive right into the program? How will you start the program? What will happen first? Design your program so that interaction begins the instant group participants enter the room.

At *Camp Sharigan,* everyone enters the room and gathers at the *stop sign.* There are no chairs and only a few tables scattered around the room. Children sit on a quilt in front of the stop sign. I dive right into a story and it is always an action story in which several children help act out the narrative. Therefore, interaction starts the minute the children walk into the room. I say, "Welcome to *Camp Sharigan* where we come to share the love of reading. Let's start this afternoon with a story. I need eight volunteers to help me with the story. Each day, we start with a story; so if you are not selected today, you'll be one of the actors selected tomorrow or the next day." Frequently in school groups, the most talented children or sometimes the best behaved children are the ones selected to come up to the front of the class. At *Camp Sharigan,* everyone gets a turn. The action is in keeping with the story, with the children acting out certain words in the story. For example, every time they hear the word *Sharigan* in the story, they hiss like a snake. The actions are simple but train the children to listen intently to the story. Therefore, the program begins with fun but structured action and the knowledge that everyone will get a turn and be included. Children are willing to wait as long as they know you are going to be fair and give everyone a turn. The story expresses two implicit rules: (1) everyone is included and treated equally – this is important in a group – and (2) we will have fun but it will be controlled, structured fun – not wild and crazy and out of control.

Designing a strong beginning is essential to effective group interaction. When a group meets for the first time, the group members will walk in through the door and bring with them their personalities, past experiences, cultural experiences, expectations of what the group is all about, past experiences with other members of the group, experiences and expectations from other groups, previous experiences with you, events of the day (good or bad), family and community background, their own self-concepts, their self-efficacy (belief that they can accomplish the tasks you place before them), and the fear or discomfort that they feel about being with a new group of people. The way you arrange the room, start the group session, and introduce the group members to your program will have a lasting effect on the interaction between the members of your group and the success and effectiveness of your program. The way you begin sets the mood and gives participants the freedom to interact or not, while your expectations of the participants give them a way to measure their success.

## Group Interaction is the Key to Successful Group Programming

Take another look; how will you build interaction into your program? *Camp Sharigan* uses a camp theme: a reading camp where we come to share the fun of reading. Colorful names, such as *camp cabins, snake pit,* and *poison ivy vine* all add to the fun reading camp theme. Do you have a theme?

How do you emphasize your theme? Can you add color, decorations, anything to add excitement and grab students' attention the minute that they walk into the room? Because *Camp Sharigan* is a portable camp, I use cloth wall hangings to help set the scene: a sunrise over a lake, a rainbow, a waterfall at the edge of the forest, and a mountain at *Mount Reading*. These wall hangings become the backdrops for each learning center. I then use props at each learning center to emphasize the theme. A crawl-in tunnel and pop-up play structure filled with soft, fuzzy fake fur snakes serve as a prop for *Sharigan's Snake Pit*. I never use rubber snakes or anything that might be construed as scary. *Sharigan* is a friendly snake used throughout the week as the camp mascot who is looking for a friend. The *snake pit* serves as the phonics station for *Camp Sharigan*. The children enjoy crawling through the tunnel and working in pairs to spell words using the letter tiles found in the *snake pit*. Hands-on props then become part of the teaching approach used at *Camp Sharigan*.

## Keep Interaction Positive

Make sure decorations are positive because you want to create a positive atmosphere. Think about how your opening will be received by participants. At a workshop where I was teaching about group-centered interventions, a counselor suggested that she would play rap music as students entered the room to set the mood for her program. You need to be careful when using music or popular symbols because the music or decorations that you use set the mood for your group and tell group members what is acceptable and unacceptable behavior. Rap music often sends a message of street behavior. Street behavior is not conducive to constructive cohesive group behavior, so be careful how you start the group. The music or decorations that you use must add to your overall goal, not detract from it.

On the other hand, think twice before just using a plain undecorated room. You would be surprised how differently students respond to a plain, bland room and a decorated room. Excitement starts the instant they walk into the room and see the decorations, but it is not always possible to decorate for every program. Therefore, you may need to build excitement in other ways. With the *Reading Orienteering Club* after school program, I designed a program that can be used in any classroom without set up or props. The teacher simply takes a notebook off the shelf and begins. Therefore, the excitement must be built into the learning center projects, through action stories, and through group activities.

Sometimes I offer the *Reading Orienteering Club* immediately following *Camp Sharigan* for students who need additional help. Occasionally, the *Reading Orienteering Club* is even held in the same classroom immediately following *Camp Sharigan,* as was the case when a little boy walked into the plain regular classroom with tables and chairs for the start of the *Reading Orienteering Club* and said, "Where's the rainbow?" Children get excited and energized by color and fun hands-on props, but if you need a program which can be used without set up and in any room, such as the *Reading Orienteering Club,* then you must find other ways to initiate interaction.

## Interaction Must Be Positive to Be Effective

Interaction is essential to the success of any program, but with the *school-based mental health approach,* interaction must also be constructive and positive. Group-centered prevention programs are usually scheduled for a certain time frame, 1 week, 6 months, a year. Because you are reversing failure with both academic and psychological goals, interaction must be positive and constructive from the instant the program begins until it ends. Group-centered interventions are not lecture sessions where you yell at students about inappropriate behavior. This does not mean rude behavior can be tolerated. Remove the student from the group for a few minutes, talk to the student individually, then return the student to the group and make sure the behavior changes. Discipline is rarely a problem at *Camp Sharigan* because the program is fun and fast paced, but, when a problem does arise, I always take the student aside to work with the student one-on-one. The student then returns to the group. The actions of one cannot be allowed to destroy the group structure or disturb the work of the entire group. Group-centered prevention programs are also not simply creative craft sessions where the children go to play or have fun. Creative ideas are good, but they must serve a purpose and they must fulfill the needs of the participants of your program. Creative ideas without purpose will not bring about change.

The *Reading Orienteering Club,* incorporates hands-on projects called *Word Masters* (Clanton Harpine 2011). These *Word Masters* help the children concentrate on learning vowel sounds by using *vowel clustering* techniques. For example, *Ollie Octopus* is a simple project made from recycled materials but the children must collect the words from the eight learning centers in order to attach *Ollie's* eight arms. I show an example of *Ollie* at the beginning of the session during the story; the children are then eager to go and collect the pieces they need from the stations in order to make their *Ollie Octopus* to take home. Each learning center stresses phonics; in this case, the many sounds for the letter O.

The way I start the session leads into the group interaction that follows. Colorful banners and props, like those in *Camp Sharigan,* are helpful but not absolutely necessary. You can build a successful program without colorful wall hangings. The key is how you start the session and what your actions tell participants you want from them.

Remember to use intrinsic rather than extrinsic motivators. *Ollie* is not an extrinsic motivator; everyone makes an octopus. Each octopus has eight arms. Anyone who shows up at the last station without eight arms is quickly assisted in making the additional arms. Everyone is included; no one is punished or left out. Even students who misbehave still make an octopus. Children soon learn to cooperate, work together, and complete their projects.

## The Need for Acceptance

Students come to a group seeking acceptance by others, a sense of accomplishment, recognition of their contributions to the group, a feeling of security, and sometimes even a feeling of power. These needs are satisfied through the interactions students have with others in the group. Students must feel safe from ridicule, embarrassment, and failure or they will not feel secure enough to rebuild their self-efficacy.

You can ensure that your group will interact in a positive, productive way by how you design and structure interactive opportunities within your program. There should be an interplay between group members and the surrounding environment in which they find themselves working. If behaviors are to be modified, group members must receive feedback that is constructive and helps the participant change their way of acting in a group (classroom) situation. Learning centers, for example, encourage both one-on-one interaction and small group interaction. Action stories and puppet plays encourage group-wide interaction. Look over the needs of your group members again (Step 4). What does your group need to be successful?

## Positive Interaction Leads to Intrinsic Motivation

Interaction is built into *Camp Sharigan's* program design by the atmosphere created and the hands-on projects used throughout the program. As with the student from the opening example, pop-up books make excellent intrinsic motivators and they also encourage group interaction. As group members work together cutting pages and assembling their pop-up books, the fun and excitement of creating a pop-up book motivates students to interact with each other. Pop-up books teach writing and spelling skills and encourage students to share their stories with the group. *Camp Sharigan* includes pop-up books to motivate reluctant students to read and write their own stories. Pop-up books provide a project that keeps the group working together and sharing ideas all week long. To be successful, interaction must be structured, positive, and supportive of the group goals. Pop-up books motivate at-risk students to tackle harder tasks than they are normally willing to attempt. Everyone in the group is working on a pop-up book; therefore, at-risk students are more willing to read out loud, ask for help, edit, rewrite, and even work with a partner as they prepare a corrected final copy of their story for their pop-up book. The excitement of the pop-up book energizes interaction between group members. The project is designed so that everyone ends up with a creative book which every student can be proud of. Therefore, the hands-on pop-up book serves both as an intrinsic week-long motivator and an initiator of group interaction. Several learning centers work on the pop-up book throughout the week; therefore, the children work together in pairs, small groups, and individually.

## Creative Does Not Mean Successful

Do not fall prey to the misconception that a creative program equals a successful program. *Camp Sharigan* and the *Reading Orienteering Club* are creative programs, but creativity alone will not teach a child to read. A creative idea that does not meet the needs of the participants does not lead to successful programming, and just because a program is creative does not make it effective. Creativity alone will also not ensure interaction. There needs to be a reason that creative ideas are included beyond just being cute, creative ideas. We must develop creative ideas in response to the needs of the group rather that just developing creative ideas for the sake of being creative.

## Create Positive Interactive Interventions

One of the key factors in the success of *Camp Sharigan* is the way in which group participants interact with each other. *Camp Sharigan* creates interactive situations. Action stories require group members to interact as they work together to act out the story, the *snake pit* creates interaction as group members work together to spell words, puppet plays require teamwork and initiate interaction both when reading and painting the puppet stage, and even the *treasure hunt maps* which help to individualize instruction also create interaction through the formulation of small groups at the learning centers. Interaction is a key factor in the success of any group program; so do not shortchange your program design by deemphasizing the need for interaction. Remember, constructive interaction will not occur automatically; you must create positive, constructive interactive situations and build them into your program design.

## Evaluate the Effectiveness of Interactive Interventions

Interaction must be developed to meet the specific needs of your group members. You must evaluate the needs of your group and then assess how well the program design meets those needs. For a program to be successful, it must meet the needs of your group participants. What works for one group may not work for another.

### *Step 7: Creating Positive Interaction*

How will you get interaction started?

How will you help group members talk with one another?




How will you help group members feel of equal importance regardless of their skill levels?




How will you make sure that more aggressive members do not tease or act negatively toward certain group members?




How will you make sure that everyone is included? What will you do if someone is not participating?

## Step 7, Design Example

In the target group from Chapter 4, I have several shy students, some students who have aggressive behavioral problems, some children who are hyperactive, and also some students who sort of fade out and forget what they are doing. I want equal participation from all of my group members. I know that such participation will not occur naturally; therefore, I plan to initiate interaction through the following activities.

*To initiate interaction at the beginning.* The attention of all students must be captured and their active participation gained at the very beginning, or their cooperation will be lost. With *Camp Sharigan*, the use of bold colors, hands-on activities, and a very quick pace initiate interaction. A summer camp scene will be created and used to make the room look inviting and help students want to get involved. The bold wall hangings and camp setting will capture the attention of the students the instant they walk in the door. I'll paint sunrise scenes, waterfalls, rainbows, and other colorful camp scenes on large ceiling to floor pieces of cloth (for complete instructions see Clanton Harpine 2010a.) I will use bold primary colors, so the room is engulfed in bright beautiful scenes. Each center is also geared toward group interaction. Each learning center will have a colorful object of focus: *Sharigan's Snake Pit* is an expandable play area with a tunnel to crawl through and a small play room in the center where children find letters to use to spell words and practice phonics sounds; *Mount Reading* is an inflatable double air mattress where children can practice spelling words and climb up to read a story; *Lake Read* has four cloth fish with Velcro hidden pouches which hide surprises that teach the children about word starters, story writing, and vowel clusters (for a more complete description see Clanton Harpine 2010a). Each of the hands-on centers has a purpose which speaks directly to the educational and psychological needs of the children participating in the program. *Camp Sharigan* is an intensive 10-hour, week-long program, which culminates at the end of the week by having children read the stories they have written for their pop-up books and by having the children work together to present a puppet play to their parents.

*To initiate verbal interaction.* Verbal interaction will be built into the program design through the use of learning centers rather than a reading group or classroom lecture approach. *Treasure hunt maps* will keep interaction going and put all students on an equal footing. *Treasure hunt maps* involve a very simple concept in which children are directed to different learning centers around the room. *Treasure hunt maps* are easy to create. Simply write clues to fit your program:

> Clue 1:    Look for the rainbow. Start at the stepping stones and cross over the rainbow
> bridge as you make your way over to the rainbow to discover what awaits you
> (Clanton Harpine 2010a).

The children look for the rainbow painting or the sign which says *Rainbow Bridge*. At the *stepping stones* the children will find the workstation notebook which gives instructions for what they are to do at this learning center today. Each map has ten clues for the ten learning centers used at *Camp Sharigan*. They simply follow the clues as they travel around the room to each learning center.

For students who feel shy in a new group setting, individual *treasure hunt maps* help them become involved in the group. The *treasure hunt maps* send the children around to all ten hands-on learning centers with no more than two or three being at a station at one time. In this way, there aren't clumps of children demanding to work together or all 20 children trying to work at the same learning center at the same time. The *treasure hunt maps* encourage children to strike out on their own; verbal interaction then happens naturally as the children mingle around the room from station to station.

*To create equality between group members.* In the group from Chapter 4, there were several students who had attention and hyperactivity problems. Hands-on learning centers will allow movement around the room, step-by-step directions at the learning centers will help students break down the task and learn to focus on completing the task one step at a time. Hands-on activities help children stay focused and also emphasize learning by doing.

*Sharigan's Snake Pit* encourages all children, even children who have trouble staying focused on a task, to break words down into their phonetic sounds so that they may learn to read and spell. It's fun to crawl into the *snake pit* and work hands-on with the letters; therefore, children who are not normally motivated to work on phonics will hurry to the *snake pit* when it is their turn. The fun nature of the learning center makes learning fun as well. Only two children are allowed to be in the snake pit at one time, which encourages interaction and teamwork as they work together to spell words.

*To control negative interactions.* The *treasure hunt maps* and the quick pace keep students involved from the minute they walk into the room until it's time to go home. The maps create equal interaction between group members and also control the actions of some of the more aggressive students. Discipline problems and teasing are rare at *Camp Sharigan*, but when they occur I simply take the child aside for some one-on-one time. I usually find that the root cause of their problem is not their behavior, but fear of failure. If I can resolve their feelings of failure and restore their confidence, the behavior takes care of itself. The group nature of *Camp Sharigan* allows for such interaction.

*To make sure everyone is included.* Each day begins with an action story. Action stories have specific words that the children act out or make noises for. For example, *Noisy the Car* (Clanton Harpine 2010a) makes all sorts of funny car noises and meets several different animals who all make noises; therefore, the children listen for their word to be read in the story so that they may participate in acting out the story. The stories help the children improve their listening skills and teach the children to interact and work cooperatively together to tell the story. The story is also a reminder to slow down and read the learning center directions because Noisy keeps getting in trouble while rushing from one place to another without taking time to read the sign. Noisy becomes a fun way to teach a classroom rule – read the directions, read all of the directions before starting to work on a project.

Bold colors motivate and get the students excited and ready to get involved. Fun stations look inviting and encourage students to interact with one another as they work the problems or complete the activity at each learning center. Step-by-step directions encourage students to work together, to interact in a positive way, and to help each other. Positive and constructive interaction is built into each step and phase of the *Camp Sharigan* program.

## Interaction is Essential for Success

Interaction is essential for effective group process, but it is also essential to unleash the therapeutic power of groups. Group-centered prevention programs must have group interaction to succeed. Therefore, give special attention to how you build interaction into your program.

## Real-World Applications

### *Observational Extensions*

Observe the students you wish to include in your new group: how do they interact together?

- Is there a domineering, demanding member of the group? What effect does this have on the group's interaction?
- Are there shy group members? What effect do shy, reserved, nonparticipating members have on the group?
- Is interaction equal among all group members?

### *Troubleshooting Checklists for Designing a New Group-Centered Program*

1. Does your intervention take into account the interaction needs of your participants?
2. Is everyone treated equally? Does everyone participate or feel free to participate? Is anyone controlling or preventing interaction? How will you tame this person's behavior in the group? Domineering personalities hinder interaction. How will you equalize group interaction throughout the group?

3. Does your program take into account the divergent personalities in your group and the ability they bring to the group to interact with others in a group setting? How will you help those who are having trouble interacting within the group? How will you get shy participants more involved?

## A Ready-to-Use Group-Centered Intervention: "Manners Please"

**Age level:** Older elementary and middle school
**Learning Objective:** To increase reading and writing skills and polish proper etiquette through hands-on activities.
**Counseling Objective:** To increase interaction and the development of the group.
**Time needed:** Divided into three 1-hour sessions

*Tips for Using this Group-Centered Intervention*: This hands-on group intervention reviews rules of etiquette in a fun way while providing an opportunity to practice reading and writing skills. This group-centered intervention works well with children, first through sixth grade. You may adapt the complexity to fit the age group.

*How to Expand into a Group-Centered Prevention Program*: One advantage of the *Manners Please* series of interventions is that they illustrate how group-centered interventions can develop around a theme. The three sessions included in this chapter may be spread out across a month, used together during a 1-week program, or expanded into a longer complete prevention program. Your school or community group may decide to host a special *Manners Please* week or month in which groups or classes practice etiquette.

This group-centered intervention also shows how you can tie learning and social skills objectives together in one intervention. The *Manners Please* interventions incorporate reading, writing, social behavior (manners), group skills, and interaction. The interventions use games, skits, and even snack time to demonstrate proper table etiquette.

These three group-centered interventions also demonstrate how to create interventions for generating interaction in a classroom setting without elaborate set up. The hands-on nature of each intervention helps keep children excited and wanting to participate. Yet these interactions are directive enough that they can be handled in a typical school classroom. The nice aspect of table and phone etiquette is that it is not construed as a criticism of how someone behaves in the classroom. You want to make sure that group-centered interventions are always positive, never a gripe session. Everyone is learning in a positive way.

This group-centered intervention is presented in 3-hour long sessions which may be combined into one long session or split into three separate sessions. Each session may also be used independently without the other two.

*Supplies needed*: Each session lists specific objectives and the supplies needed.

## Session 1: Would You Like to Join Us for Dinner?

Goal: To teach basic table manners and dining skills.
Learning Objectives:

1. Summarize table etiquette in order to promote polite table manners.
2. Identify proper placement of table settings – silverware, plates, cups, etc.
3. Utilize skills learned to demonstrate proper table etiquette during a simple meal.
4. Practice writing invitations.

Counseling Objective: To initiate interaction in a new group.
Time needed: 1 hour
Supplies:

1. Placemats: On a large piece of paper upon which to trace outline of plate, two glasses, bread plate, salad plate, two forks, two spoons, knife, and napkin. Placing each item in its proper location on the place mat (photocopy and have ready for distribution).
2. Markers or crayons.
3. Paper plates, cups, plastic ware to set the table.
4. Snack foods and beverage for practice at the table, if desired (Plan a snack that uses table utensils so that children may practice.).
5. Table Quiz questions and a basket for children to draw questions from.

Preparations: Have tables and chairs arranged before children arrive (round tables are nice if available but a cluster of student desks work fine as well). Have crayons or markers sitting in the center of each table. Have placemats ready – one for each child. Decide on food to be served and have food ready.

Step 1: As children arrive, give each child a placemat and tell them to select a table and to begin decorating their placemat. Young children may make bold decorations, older children may make elaborate decorations; the idea is for all children to personalize their placemat and give an interactive beginning.

Step 2: Talk about placemats: placemats remind us how to set the table. Give each child an opportunity to show their artwork and tell about their placemat.

Step 3: Play *Table Quiz* game. Children draw a question out of the basket. Older children will be able to read the question on their own and answer. Younger children may require assistance in reading the question. (See attached list of ten questions/answers.)

Step 4: Pass out paper plates, cups, and plasticware one at a time. Discuss where each item should be placed on the placemat. Review table etiquette – napkin, passing food, etc.

Step 6: Once table settings are complete, select a waiter/waitress for each table to pass out snacks and practice eating using table manners.

Step 7: End the session by passing out a paper invitation for next week. Have students write an invitation to a friend (If you are using this program in the school, you might consider inviting another class to join you for the next session and writing invitations to that class). If time permits, children may color and decorate the invitations.

**Table Quiz Game**

1. What should you do if you spill a glass of milk on the table?
   A: Say, "I'm sorry." Then help clean up your mess.

2. What do you do if you drop your fork on the floor?
   A: If you're in a restaurant, leave the fork on the floor and ask for another fork. Remember to say thank you and please.
   If you are at home, ask if you may go and get another fork.

3. Is it polite to burp at the table?
   A: Never, but if it happens by accident, say "excuse me."

4. If you and your family are at a fancy restaurant and the table is set with two forks, which fork do you use first?
   A: Start with the fork farthest from the plate. That is the salad fork.

5. When you pass food around the table, which direction do you pass the serving dish?
   A: To the right.

6. When you have finished eating where do you put your silverware?
   A: On your plate.

7. If you have to leave the table before dinner is finished, what do you do?
   A: Ask if you may be excused from the table by saying, "May I please be excused?" Leave your silverware on your plate. Place your napkin in your chair. Push your chair in at the table. Remember to be polite.

8. How do you hold your fork?
   A: Hold your fork with the same hand you write with – right or left. You hold a fork or spoon the same way you hold a pencil.

9. Is it OK to talk while you chew?
   A: No. Always chew with your mouth closed. Never talk when there is food in your mouth.

10. Should we watch television while we eat?
    A: No. Turn off the television and the computer during meal time. Let dinner time be family time.

## Session 2: When You Call on the Telephone

Goal: To teach basic telephone etiquette.
Learning Objectives:

1. Summarize phone etiquette in order to promote polite and safe use of the telephone.
2. Identify proper way to answer the telephone and take messages.
3. Utilize skills learned to demonstrate proper telephone etiquette.

Counseling Objective: Group development as everyone practices telephone skits and discusses proper etiquette.

Time needed: 1 hour

Supplies:

1. Stiff paper for making paper cell phones (use paper cutter and cut paper to make a cell phone for each child – cut an 8 × 2-in. piece of stiff paper for each child), markers and/or crayons for designing phones (paper phones work better than real cell phones – real phones are too tempting to play with)
2. Scripts for telephone role plays
3. Telephones to practice with (old desk telephones work best)

Preparations: Have tables and chairs arranged before children arrive (round tables are nice if available but even a classroom arrangement with desks will work fine). Have crayons or markers sitting in the center of each table. Children will work on designing their own cell phone as they wait for everyone to arrive.

Step 1: As children arrive, give each child a paper cell phone and tell them to select a table and to begin decorating their cell phone. Young children may make bold decorations; older children might make elaborate decorations; the idea is for all children to personalize their cell phone and give an orderly, fun beginning.

Step 2: Be prompt. Start on time.

Step 3: Give children an opportunity to show off their phones. Talk about telephones and being polite when we talk on the telephone.

Step 4: Have two volunteers read the phone script and role play using the desk telephones or paper cell phones (do not use working telephones).


*Phone Script #1: What Not to Do* (**Names can be for girls or guys**)

(Erin picks up the telephone and pretends to dial. Make a phone ringing noise; Chris answers the telephone.)

Chris: Hello!

Erin: Hey, what's up?

Chris: Oh … not much … and you? (Chris should sound puzzled because he/she doesn't know who is calling.)

Erin: Why aren't you here? You're late. Aren't you coming?

Chris: Well … I …

Erin: Come on, come on, we've got to go. We're going to be late.

Chris: Who is this? Go where? Are you sure you have the right number?

Step 5: Talk about what Chris should have said when someone didn't give their name on the telephone. Have the same two volunteers role play script #2 (use the same volunteers for scripts 1 and 2 because you do not want someone left with the stigma of doing the conversation wrong).

**Phone Script #2: Identifying the Caller**

(Erin picks up the telephone and pretends to dial. Make a phone ringing noise; Chris answers the phone.)

Chris:  Hello!
Erin:   Hey, what's up?
Chris:  May I ask, who you are calling?
Erin:   Oh, I'm calling Jody.
Chris:  I'm sorry, there's no one by that name at this address. Perhaps you have the wrong number.
Erin:   Oh, I'm sorry. Thank you. (Click – both hang up phone.)

Step 6: Have everyone find a partner. Use their cardboard cell phones and practice identifying the caller as in script #2.
Step 7: Select two more volunteers to come up front to the desk telephones and role play Script #3.

**Phone Script #3: Who Is This?**

(Jody picks up telephone and pretends to dial. Make a phone ringing noise; Ty answers the phone.)

Ty:     Hello!
Jody:   Is Sam there?
Ty:     I'm sorry, there's no one at this number named Sam.
Jody:   Who is this?
Ty:     I'm sorry, what number did you dial?
Jody:   Who are you? What's your name?
Ty:     I'm sorry, do you know what number you dialed?
Jody:   Who is this? Will you let me speak to Sam? (Jody begins to sound rude.)
Ty:     I'm sorry, I believe you have dialed incorrectly. (Click, Ty hangs up the telephone.)

Step 8: Talk about how Ty handled the caller. Explain why you should never give your name if you do not know the caller. You want to be polite, but you do not give information that is unsafe to give to strangers. Select new volunteers and role play script #4.

**Script #4: Is your Mom or Dad home?**

(Jody picks up the telephone and pretends to dial. Make a phone ringing noise; Ty answers the phone.)

Ty:     Hello!
Jody:   Is your mom or dad there?
Ty:     No, they're at work.

Step 9: Stop and discuss why it is not safe to tell someone you do not know that you are home alone. Discuss how you should respond if someone comes to the door as well. The rule is: Never open the door. On the telephone, the rule is: Never tell anyone that you are home alone.

Step 10: Have the same volunteers demonstrate the proper phone conversation.

## Script #5: Is your Mom or Dad home? (The right way.)

Ty:     Hello!
Jody:   Is your mom or dad there?
Ty:     I'm sorry, they can't come to the telephone at the moment. May I take a message, please?
Jody:   No, I'll call back later.
Ty:     Who may I say called?

Step 11: Have everyone practice: "Who is this" and "Is your mom or dad home?" strategies with their paper cell phones.

Step 12: Select two new volunteers and practice the proper way to initiate a call and proper way to end a telephone call.

## Script #6: Proper Phone Etiquette

Lu:     Hello.
Cary:   May I speak with Lu, please? (Even if you know that the person on the phone is Lu.)
Lu:     This is Lu speaking.
Cary:   Hi, Lu, this is Cary.
Lu:     Hi, Cary, it's great to hear from you today.
Cary:   I was calling to see if you wanted to go to the lake with my family.
Lu:     That sounds great. I'll have to ask my parents. (Parents are not home.) May I call you back later after I discuss it with them?
Cary:   Sure, we're going on Saturday. We plan to leave at 9:00 a.m., and we will return by 7:30 p.m. My dad is taking us out in our boat. It will be a lot of fun. I hope you can come.
Lu:     So do I, but I'll have to talk this over with my parents and check our family schedule. I'll call you back as soon as possible. Thanks again for inviting me.
Cary:   I'll wait to hear from you. Bye.
Lu:     Bye and thanks for calling.

Step 13: Have everyone practice making a correct call without saying that their parents are not home and one showing how to handle an invitation over the phone. If time permits, you may have volunteers come forward to role play for the entire group.

## Session 3: You're Invited

Goal: To teach basic oral and written etiquette for invitations.
Learning Objectives:

1. Summarize oral and written etiquette used in sending invitations.
2. Identify proper invitation and thank you note etiquette.
3. Use skills learned to demonstrate proper letter writing techniques.

Counseling Objective: Developing group skills and kindness toward others.
Time needed: 1 hour
Supplies:

1. Plain white blank invitation cards – two for each participant
2. Paper, ink pens, and pencils for writing

Preparations: Have tables and chairs arranged before children arrive (round tables are nice if available). Have crayons or markers sitting in the center of each table.

Step 1: As children arrive, give each child a plain white blank invitation and tell them to select a table and to begin decorating their invitation. Young children may make bold decorations, older children may make elaborate decorations; the idea is for all children to personalize their invitations and set the stage for personal interaction.

Step 2: Be prompt. Start on time. Welcome everyone.

Step 3: Use writing paper, pens, and pencils to write invitations. Have children at each table plan a party. They may set a theme for their party. Plan decorations, food, games, even set a day and time for the party. Next, on scratch paper, have children write an invitation to the party. Talk about what should be included in an invitation: date, time, place, theme or type of party, whether or not people are expected to bring gifts, and why you should include an RSVP. Set up an "Editor's Desk." You can even make a sign. Have children bring their invitations to the Editor's Desk for a grammar and spelling check as well as proper invitation etiquette.

Step 4: Practice a phone invitation.

Skit (Have Cindy call Judy. Cindy dials the telephone and pretends to make phone ring.)

Judy:   Hello!
Cindy:  May I speak with Judy?
Judy:   This is Judy.
Cindy:  Judy, this is Cindy from school. I'm having a pajama party for my birthday on Friday, and I would like to know if you can come. The party starts at 5:00 p.m. We're going to grill hot dogs in the back yard. Then, we're going to watch movies and play games all night. I'll open my birthday presents at midnight. You don't have to bring a present, but if you want to that's fine. Even

though no one's planning to sleep, bring a sleeping bag, pillow, toothbrush, all of those bedtime things. We'll have breakfast at 9:00 a.m. We're having pancakes and strawberries from the garden. Parents are to pick up at 10:00 a.m. on Saturday. My mom and dad will be home supervising the entire time, and mom said to have any parents who have questions give her a call at 803-642-0010.

Judy: That sounds great, but I'll have to check and see if we have plans. I'll check with my mom and call you back.

Cindy: Fantastic, I hope you can come.

Judy: So do I. I'll call as soon as I know for sure.

Cindy: Talk with you soon. Bye.

Judy: Bye, and thank you for inviting me. I'm really excited. (Click)

Step 5: Go back to the party that each table planned and write final copies of their invitations to the party. You may actually plan a party or just practice writing invitations. Do a final edit on final copy. Remember to include all of the details an invitation should include.

Step 6: Allow several people to read their invitations.

Step 7: Next, pretend you were invited to the party that your table planned. How would you write a thank you note for the party? What would you say? Use your second card and write a thank you note.

# Chapter 8
# Self-Efficacy: The Learning Component in Schools

*A first grader was enrolled in my program because his parents were concerned about him doing well in school. The little boy, who had a speech problem, was difficult to understand when he spoke, and he was extremely reluctant to interact with other children because he feared that they would tease him. The end of Camp Sharigan coincided with the school sending home the student's first report card. The little boy received high marks and was actually on the honor roll. The school had diagnosed the little boy with attention deficit hyperactivity disorder (ADHD). ADHD combined with speech difficulties had caused the school to label the child as learning-disabled. He was therefore, according to the school, graded on a different scale to preserve his self-esteem. When I tested the student at the close of Camp Sharigan, he was still reading below grade level. I recommended that he continue in my after school program. The parents were confused, "How could he be on the honor roll and still be reading below his grade level?" The school had, in essence, sentenced this child to failure. He could not read and was not improving through remedial programs in the school. Without outside intervention, the student would most likely have become another unfortunate statistic and example of academic failure and dropping out of school before graduation. The parents did not have the education or ability to help their child at home. The child needed more than simply a one-week program; he needed an ongoing year-long program that could help him continue to improve and work up to his full potential. Six months into the Reading Orienteering Club program, the first grader began to feel more confident and also began to make real progress in reading.*

Self-efficacy is the internal control mechanism (confidence and intrinsic desire) that allows students to succeed academically and achieve psychological well-being and happiness (Taylor et al. 2000). Children must have positive self-efficacy if they are to learn, but simply distorting grading scales under the disguise of preserving self-esteem will not help students learn (Baumeister et al. 2005). Self-esteem and self-efficacy are not the same, and it is self-efficacy, not self-esteem, that helps students learn (Bandura 1977; Clanton Harpine 2008).

Clanton Harpine, *Group-Centered Prevention Programs for At-Risk Students*,
DOI 10.1007/978-1-4419-7248-4_8, © Springer Science+Business Media, LLC 2011

## How Does Self-Efficacy Work?

Self-efficacy begins in early infancy. Positive self-efficacy requires a family environment that encourages curiosity, allows children to explore and master new tasks, teaches coping skills for problems, supports persistence, and provides new activities with positive peer groups (Schunk and Pajares 2005). This need continues as the child enters school. Teachers who support the development of positive self-efficacy must create experiences for their students which also encourage curiosity, allow for exploration, teach new skills, model coping behaviors for problems, lay the groundwork for persistence with difficult tasks, and provide group activities which foster positive peer interaction.

A student's self-efficacy includes the student's ability to use talents and skills to cope with the classroom's problems and demands. To increase self-efficacy, the student must have positive experiences coupled with the necessary skill-building activities to establish a feeling of success (Bandura 1995). Mandated testing, test preparation booklets, a bombardment of worksheets, or extrinsic rewards (prizes, points, or candy) given for good behavior or for completing seat work do not teach the principles needed to develop positive self-efficacy or lead to academic competence (Sternberg et al. 1997; Urdan and Turner 2005). Students who have low self-efficacy do not value learning and consequently do not exert a great deal of effort, which ultimately results in their receiving little satisfaction from the learning experience (Bandura et al. 2001). Learning is neither important to them nor enjoyable.

Self-efficacy involves choice, persistence, and coping with stress. If your program design focuses on rebuilding self-efficacy, then it must combine positive prevention (Seligman and Csikzentmihalyi 2000) with academic and social competence (Brigman and Webb 2007) and positive development and mental well-being (Catalano et al. 2003). Therefore, an effective program design must include not only intrinsic motivators, interaction, and cohesion, but also a means to rebuild self-efficacy. Incorporating necessary skill-building is the key (Bandura 1997).

## Why is Skill-Building So Important with Self-Efficacy?

Bandura (1977) states that we must teach the necessary skills for learning a task if we are to rebuild a student's belief that he or she can succeed in the classroom. Students must be taught the skills necessary to achieve learning a particular concept, such as teaching phonetic decoding skills in order to help children learn to read. In reading, the student's ability to use phonological knowledge to decode and read letter symbols written on a page and then ascribe meaning to those letter symbols is essential. Students cannot and will not learn to read unless they are taught the necessary phonetic skills (Foorman et al. 2003).

# How Can You Design Interventions that Rebuild Self-Efficacy?

Self-efficacy is the mechanism that a program must have to enhance and encourage intrinsic motivation and increase academic performance. The best way to increase self-efficacy is to develop an environment which appeals to the interests of the students while still at the same time teaching the necessary skills to become competent (Bandura 1997).

*Hands-on Learning is Best.* Hands-on activities (games, puzzles, crafts) work well in the classroom or in an after school program to build self-efficacy and academic competence. Skill building through intrinsic hands-on learning centers then becomes an essential component of our prevention program format.

An example of how hands-on activities at learning centers can be used to teach both educational and social skills comes from the *Rainbow Bridge* learning center. The children were painting their puppet stage. One group wanted to paint a field of flowers, but they did not have the skills to paint flowers. As one child explained, "we want our flowers to look like flowers." I proceeded to teach one child each day a very simple flower to paint. It was then that child's responsibility to teach the next child who came to the station. We made handprint tulips, cotton swab star flowers, thumb print hyacinths, and fingertip daisies. The children were very proud of their puppet stage because, as one child explained, "it's not just a mess of painting; it's a real picture." By teaching simple step-by-step procedures for making flowers, the children were able to learn a skill and learn to work as a team to complete a project of which they could be very proud of. There was no competition; everyone was working together. On the last day, when children had free painting time to paint the cover for their "I Am Special" booklet, the children, without prompting, painted flower gardens on their covers showing the different types of flowers they had learned to paint.

*Learning Centers Combine Individualized Learning and Teamwork.* Students learn more and are more likely to retain what they learn when they are actively engaged in learning (Ladd and Dinella 2009). This has been shown to be true for both short-term and long-term retention and understanding (Buhs et al. 2006). Hands-on activities at learning centers provide this engagement.

An example of a third grade student having problems staying focused on task in the classroom illustrates how self-efficacy works. He was diagnosed with ADHD and was reading at the first grade level, although I thought that he might be able to read at the second grade level if he could stay focused and concentrate on the task. The student had a difficult time moving from station to station at *Camp Sharigan*. He would simply wander off and sit down and look at a book. While I was glad he was looking at a book, I needed him to stay focused on the task in order to improve his reading skills. Following *Camp Sharigan* the student entered the *Reading Orienteering Club* after school year-long program. Some students need more than just a 1-week program. The *Reading Orienteering Club* (Clanton Harpine 2011) uses the same hands-on learning center format as *Camp Sharigan*. It uses the same *four-step method* for learning tricky new words, emphasizes *vowel clustering*, uses only intrinsic motivation, and combines learning and counseling techniques into the same group-centered program format. The *Reading Orienteering Club* further expands the *Camp Sharigan* concept into a year-long program for those who need more intense remedial help.

Two months into the *Reading Orienteering Club* program, the student began to make his way to every learning center station, just like other students. Working in a group setting, watching and modeling after other students was helping the student learn to work within the program. At 3 months, he began to show progress in reading and definite improvement in staying focused on the task during the 2-hours after school program.

Approximately 6 months into the *Reading Orienteering Club* program, the student arrived one day displaying attention-focus problems. At his first learning center, he struggled to read an easy, vowel-clustered story. I noticed that he was struggling to concentrate, so, instead of encouraging him to work the *challenge step* (each station at the *Reading Orienteering Club* has a challenge step to invite students to push a little harder; students choose to accept or not accept the challenge), I encouraged him to move on and see what awaited him at the next learning center. Instead of giving up and wandering off task (staring off into space), as had been his previous behavior, he went on to see what the next learning center would ask him to do. On that particular day, his second learning center offered an even longer, more challenging story to read. The student sat down at the second learning center and tackled the second story with more determination and succeeded, even completing the *challenge step*, and moved on to the third learning center with a smile. He didn't give up or lose focus. He believed in himself. He knew that he could do the task placed before him (self-efficacy), and he was willing to meet the challenge. By allowing him to move along to the next learning center instead of forcing him to complete the challenge step, I allowed him to readjust his thinking and meet the demands of the program.

With this student, hands-on activities in a group-centered learning center structure made all the difference. Learning centers organized the learning tasks so that the student could approach each task one step at a time.

The student's mother had remarked several times that the student did not like to read; it was simply too difficult a task for him. She marveled at how he would so willingly read story after story in the after school program. I explained to her, "that's part of the *Camp Sharigan* concept." The program combines one-on-one learning center assistance by having a helper at each station with the excitement and motivation of being a part of a group. By placing the learning centers in a group-centered format, the participants receive the benefit of both one-on-one assistance and the benefits of being a member of a positive, constructive group as well. One-on-one tutoring cannot match the power of group process. Yet, simple groups do not provide the individual instruction often needed by at-risk children and teens. Group-centered interventions combine one-on-one tutoring and group process together in a learning center focused group-centered prevention program.

*Self-efficacy must be intertwined with intrinsic motivation.* Increasing a student's self-efficacy leads to an increase in long-term intrinsic motivation. The truth is that you cannot build positive self-efficacy without intrinsic motivation (Deci and Ryan 1985), and students will not be intrinsically motivated unless they have positive self-efficacy (Bandura 1977). Self-efficacy exerts pressure on motivation by determining choice of activities, how much effort and persistence are put forth, the quality of thinking and decision making, and the emotional reactions (stress and anxiety) affecting the student's overall wellness (Bandura 1997). Intrinsic motivation and self-efficacy work hand in hand in the classroom and in group-centered prevention programs.

## Self-Efficacy Helps Reduce Classroom Problems

Once rebuilt, self-efficacy empowers students to take control over their actions in the classroom. Students stop avoiding difficult tasks and begin to accept personal responsibility (self-regulation) for their actions and motivation to complete assigned work. Self-efficacy also enhances a student's ability to focus on a task. Doubt and uncertainty weaken the student's ability to accomplish a classroom task. When you choose an intervention format, it is important that the format meet the participants' needs. Three important psychological needs are self-determination, competence, and relatedness. These provide the basis for learning and developing as a healthy person (Ryan and Deci 2000). As you design your program, you will need to establish how you plan to convey information or teach skills through your program in order to rebuild self-efficacy.

### *Step 8: Creating Learning Centers*

What subject or skill set are you incorporating into your program?

What skills do you plan for the students to learn?

How will you teach these skills through learning centers?

What is the best way to teach the material at the learning center?

## Step 8, Design Example

At *Camp Sharigan*, I teach reading because reading is so closely tied to psychological wellness. The goal is to help at-risk students improve their reading skills so that they can return to class and read at grade level.

*Subject or Skill Set being Taught.* Groups have been identified as the most effective way for teaching reading (National Reading Panel 2000). Schools subscribe to ability-level reading groups and one-on-one reading tutoring for at-risk readers, but school reading groups and traditional pull-out reading tutoring do not work with at-risk readers (Foorman et al. 2003). Hands-on learning techniques instead of worksheets have proved to be more successful with at-risk children (Morris et al. 2000). Therefore, I sought a different group approach than the methods used in the classroom. I wanted to use hands-on learning centers to teach reading and social skills. To be effective, each learning center should be positive, allow for a sense of control, encourage persistence, provide choices, show success, and encourage commitment. Each learning center should also involve a hands-on activity to help engage students and stress group cohesion and working together cooperatively. I incorporated the concept of *camp guides*, helpers or tutors at each learning center station. *Camp guides* help the children read the station directions, work the problem, or complete the activity. By incorporating *camp guides,* I combined the advantages of one-on-one tutoring with the advantages of group process to create a group-centered prevention program.

*Skills Students will Learn.* Research indicates that understanding the interrelationships between sounds and letter symbols is more effective in teaching reading than memorizing weekly word lists or completing reading worksheets (Rayner et al. 2001). Students must understand the interrelationships between written symbols (letters) and phonological sounds. Teaching reading should begin with teaching phonics (Rayner et al. 2001). Therefore, I wanted to combine reading, writing, and spelling into a comprehensive phonics-based, hands-on, learning center structured group-centered prevention program. Memorizing word lists, guessing, and work-sheets would not be used in the program.

*Way in which I will teach skills.* *Camp Sharigan* uses ten learning centers. I incorporate skill-building into the learning centers at *Camp Sharigan* by using:

1. *Pop-up Books*: The children make a pop-up book at the *camp cabin* station to encourage them to read, follow directions, and write their own stories. Often children stall and have trouble when told to sit down and write. The pride of writing a book motivates children to want to read and write. A pop-up book with increasing steps of difficulty will allow high achieving and struggling students to work on the same project by allowing students to select the number of pop-up pages for their book. The excitement of making their own pop-up book encourages children to work on grammar, spelling, and handwriting skills in order to write the best book possible.

2. *Puppet Plays*: Working together as a team at the *rainbow bridge* to present a puppet play encourages children to tackle harder reading material, practice using a dictionary, and also motivates students to read orally. Puppet plays integrate the six motivators by providing a positive group activity in which everyone can participate regardless of their reading level or age level and by encouraging persistence and helping children to challenge themselves to learn new words and read harder material. The practice and presentation of a puppet play emphasize self-efficacy. Oral reading skills are important.

3. *Word Games*: The *friendship tree* learning center offers a new word game each day which stresses phonics, learning new words, and word recognition of commonly confused words, such as 'there' and 'their.' Turning spelling, phonics, and reading into a game allows children to develop necessary skills without the drudgery of normal classroom worksheets or lectures (Rayner et al. 2001). Children read directions to play the game. Then, along with their *camp guide,* play word games that emphasize phonics and *vowel clustering*.

4. *Storytelling*: All sessions start with action stories that allow the children to act out characters in the stories. They also have to use their listening skills to hear their cue in the story. Oral action stories encourage teamwork by sharing responsibility and learning to help each other. Sometimes the story is continued at *Lake Read* where children can then write their own endings for a story or write their very own story using *story starters* found in the fish at *Lake Read*. Through action stories and *story starters*, the children begin to believe in their ability to write. Their self-efficacy is restored.

5. *Capturing Tricky Words*: At the *camp library* the *poison ivy vine* teaches children to think of words missed as *tricky words captured*. The reversal in concepts helps strengthen the rebuilding of self-efficacy and positive thinking and helps everyone learn to read and spell difficult vocabulary words. At one site, the children captured 625 words. The children process each word captured using the *4-step method* (Clanton Harpine 2010a). The *poison ivy vine* stresses the six motivators by emphasizing success for everyone and encouraging everyone

to learn new *tricky words* as they continue to work on sometimes difficult reading material within the fun nature of the game.

6. *Reading and Following Directions to Complete a Project*: Following step-by-step directions helps children work on comprehension skills. Hands-on projects at the *campfire* reinforce the six motivators by strengthening and encouraging children's commitment to learning by making learning fun and by allowing children to choose the level of difficulty of a project.

7. *Building Words*: Using word starters helps children learn new words. Encouraging children to work together as a team is also an excellent social skills motivator. *Mount Reading* keeps children rushing to work on spelling words every single day. Spelling is a totally different cognitive process than reading. Children need to practice both skills.

8. *Oral and Silent Reading*: New books are available each day at the *stop sign* to encourage chapter book reading. *Camp guides* help the children read and capture new words. Chapter books build confidence and the children are given free books to take home, not as a prize or reward, but as a motivator to keep reading. Everyone receives a book.

9. *"You're the Author" – Comprehension Skill-building Activities*: The children work at the *tent* as authors and editors, because reading and writing silly stories is an excellent way to teach comprehension. Writing stresses the six motivators by emphasizing commitment and teamwork in a positive group atmosphere and by showing the children's success and progress through stories which increase in difficulty day after day. Grammar and spelling are emphasized to build self-efficacy.

10. *Phonics*: All reading game activities incorporate phonics, but *Sharigan's snake pit* is by far the biggest success with phonics. By offering children a positive, fun way to practice remedial phonics skills, *Sharigan's snake pit* not only motivates children but also provides necessary skill building for self-efficacy. There are no correct or incorrect answers and there is no competition. The children work together as a team to practice and learn phonics.

*Best Way to Teach.* I have found learning centers to be one of the most effective ways to teach children of any age on any subject. Because I work with at-risk readers, I use helpers at the learning centers. Fourth and fifth graders, middle school youth, high school teens, college students, and adult community volunteers can be helpers. Because there is a written program packet, with the program content contained in the learning center instructions, the helpers' expertise does not matter. The program packet does the teaching.

## Ready-to-Use Program Packets

By using a written ready-to-use program packet, school-based programmers can develop hands-on learning center activities using intrinsic motivators to help build more effective evidence-based group prevention programs that foster school-based mental health. *Camp Sharigan* is just one case example of how such techniques can be applied. As you develop your program, ask yourself if your program will be used by others or whether you will be using the program at more than one site. If the answer is yes, then writing your program as a ready-to-use program packet (as we are doing in the step-by-step process in this book) will enable you to use this program at multiple sites with assurance.

Using step-by-step program packets allows replication and consistency with evidence-based research programs (Fagan et al. 2008). The *Camp Sharigan* program has ready-to-use step-by-step directions for each learning center (Clanton Harpine 2010a). The exact same program can be used over and over at numerous sites and with different facilitators. The program stays the same because the learning center written instructions contain the change agents and teaching principles.

By providing learning centers with ready-to-use written directions, we can ensure high-quality program implementation. Through written program packets, evidence-based programs can be replicated as intended and thereby generate the same results regardless of the setting or facilitator. If the program for change and motivators are written into the learning center directions, then consistency can be ensured.

Children need both cognitive skills and motivation to do well in school (Pintrich and Schunk 2002). By reversing the pattern of lowered self-efficacy, rebuilding their self-determination to learn, and giving children the freedom to decide to learn, we can renew their ability to advance in school and succeed in life (Bandura et al. 2001). Adding choices and freedom to work at one's own pace proved essential in the *Camp Sharigan* program.

In my year-long test of the *Camp Sharigan* program, using a randomly selected sample, students at *Camp Sharigan* not only outscored children in the control group (who participated in a typical classroom style program) but were still showing positive results 1 year later (Clanton Harpine and Reid 2009a). Repeated testing of the *Camp Sharigan* program at multiple test sites has continued to show student improvement at each test site (Clanton Harpine 2005a; Clanton Harpine 2007a; Clanton Harpine and Reid 2009b). Because the program has been written as a program packet with ready-to-use learning center instructions, the program is the same each time it is implemented, regardless of learning center helpers and program director. The skill-building content of the program, the group process techniques for change, and the intrinsic motivators, are all in the written program. That is one of the major features of this approach to designing prevention programs. Most programs describe what you should do in a manual, however, execution of the program is up to the group leader. A written ready-to-use program packet ensures that evidence-based programs are implemented as designed because everything is written into a ready-to-use program.

You are now at the point of writing your learning center instructions. First, write instructions for the skills to be learned and then add the counseling aspects. The group-centered intervention, *The Grumps on Vacation*, included in this chapter demonstrates one method for writing learning center instructions.

# Real-World Applications

## *Observational Extensions*

Observe students in a classroom or instructional setting.

- How can you tell that students are learning?
- Must students take a test before you can tell whether students are learning the concepts being taught or not?
- Do students have a way to measure their success in the classroom each day?
- How would you change the group that you are observing to build in measures of success so that students can chart their academic improvement and progress?

## *Troubleshooting Checklists for Designing a New Group-Centered Program*

1. Is it clear from your program description what you are teaching or what you want the students to learn?
2. Does your program design include some form of pre- and post-testing in order to measure the success of your program?
3. Have you built in measures so that students can see their own improvement?
4. Are you using measures of improvement other than testing? If not, can you go back and build into your program measures of improvement that are not tests? Do you incorporate daily measures so that students can chart their own progress?

## *A Ready-to-Use Group-Centered Intervention: "The Grumps on Vacation"*

**Age level:** Third grade through eighth grade
**Learning Objective:** To increase comprehension when reading through hands-on activities.
**Counseling Objective:** To enhance acceptance of other people's work and talents.
**Time needed:** 1–2 weeks, depending how many pages of the story you choose to do a day. You can use the story for a 1-day activity, across a 2-week period, completing three pages a day, or expand the project into a month-long activity.

*Tips for Using this Group-Centered Intervention*:  This group-centered intervention works well with older elementary children and middle school youth, especially those who struggle with comprehension. By encouraging readers to draw details pertaining to what they read, it teaches children to read and remember details in a story.

*How to Expand into a Group-centered Prevention Program*: This project can also serve as a story starter for a story writing assignment. Have students create stories about the Grump family or create other stories based on a single word. When finished, students can staple the book together to take home. You also might arrange for your students to read and share the story with a younger group of children.

*Supplies needed*: A copy of the story for each student, markers, colored pencils, or crayons

1. Set up a learning center where students can go and work independently or set aside a special time for your group to work on the story.
2. Being an illustrator will train students to look for details in each page of a story.

## *The Grumps on Vacation*

Welcome to our story corner. You are going to be the illustrator for our story, *The Grumps on Vacation*. Illustrators may use pencils, pens, markers, crayons, or even paints. Use the supplies provided to illustrate the book. Remember, picture books show the details of a story through pictures. Read the entire story. Then, go back and read each page a second time as you illustrate. Editors often specify what they want an illustrator to draw. Your assignment for each page is in brackets at the bottom of the page. You're the illustrator; go to work. You will not be able to do all of the drawings at once; so take your time and do your best. Art skills do not matter; we are looking for details from the story. So have fun.

### Page 1

Far away in a bamboo forest lived a family of Grumps. There was a Mama Grump, a Papa Grump, a big brother Grump, a big sister Grump, and a baby sister Grump. There was also a Grandma and Grandpa Grump. Grandma and Grandpa lived across the mountains and only visited once a year.

The Grump family lived in a yellow cave house with blue shutters at the top of a tall hill with a dirt path that led from their front door to the street below. Sarcasm Boulevard went right past the Grump's house and on into Grumpville where you could take the highway to Grumpity City.

[The first page could show the Grump family, a family of panda bears, all clustered together at the mailbox smiling and posing as if for a picture. Include yellow cave house at the top of hill with winding path down to the street below.]

### Page 2

There was just one store in Grumpville, but Uncle Grump's store had just about everything. Uncle Grump had milk, bread, nails, feed for the chickens, and grump juice for the car.

Uncle Grump's motto was that if he didn't have what you were looking for, you just plain didn't need it. Therefore, you'd best do without or shop for something else.

It took the whole afternoon to get to Grumpity City by grumpmobile, so the Grumps didn't go to Grumpity very often. The Grumps learned to make do with whatever Uncle Grump had on hand.

Once a month, if there were at least five letters, a letter carrier was dispatched out to deliver mail to Grumpville. If there weren't five letters, then the fine people of Grumpville had to wait another month before their mail would be delivered.

"Ya-Hoo, it's the Grumpity City mail" said the letter carrier as she placed the letter in the mail box. Letters were carved onto pieces of wood in Grumpville for paper and pens did not exist. Having to carve your letter instead of writing it tended to keep correspondence short and to the point.

[Draw a picture of Grumpville.]

## Page 3

"Ya-Hoo to you too," said Papa Grump. "Come quick everyone," said Papa, "it's a letter from Grandma and Grandpa."

Just as Papa was saying "Grandpa," big brother Grump slid down the path from the front door to the mailbox. Big sister was right behind him, but she sort of bumped along instead of sliding. Big sister didn't like going too fast downhill. Baby Grump stood at the top of the hill crying. Mama Grump swept baby Grump up and scurried down the hill to hear the news.

[A picture with Papa Grump standing at the mailbox waving the letter boards back and forth over his head. Show brother and sister Grump sliding down the path, brother going fast, sister bumping along, and baby standing at the top jumping up and down. Mama could be running to get baby Grump.]

## Page 4

"Grandma and Grandpa Grump are coming to our house for summer vacation," said Papa "they're even coming on the grumpplane this year instead of driving for 2 days straight in their dilapidated old grumpmobile."

"Thank goodness," said Mama. "I worry about them so when they try to make that long drive over the mountains."

"Yes, and they're coming next week," said Papa.

"Oh dear," said Mama, "We have to clean house."

"Why do we have to clean?" said brother. "Grandma and Grandpa are coming to see us not the house."

"That's beside the point," said Mama, "clean house we shall."

"I like my room messy," said big sister Grump, "a messy room has character."

"Then, your room shall have no character," said Mama.

[Draw a picture showing the messy rooms.]

**Page 5**

"What about baby Grump? Doesn't she have to clean? It's her room too."

Big sister and baby Grump shared a bedroom. According to big sister, baby Grump was the only one who ever played with the toys and therefore should have to do all of the cleaning.

"Everyone will pick up toys," said Mama, "regardless of who was playing with them last. When all of the toys are put away, we'll blow the dust out of the rooms, wash the shutters, and…"

Papa went off to hide and read the newsboard. The thought of cleaning always made Papa tired and in much need of rest. The newsboard gave all the latest news from Grumpity City. Grumpville received one newsboard a month with the mail. The newsboard would be passed from house to house until everyone in Grumpville was given a chance to read the news. Papa was taking his turn right now.

[Show baby Grump sitting in the middle of the mess in her bedroom looking as pleased as punch, while Papa lies underneath a big shady tree with a glass of lemonade, fan in one hand, and newsboard in the other.]

**Page 6**

Big brother decided to get his room clean before dinner. Brother stacked everything in a sky-high, slightly tottering tower right inside his closet door. Brother ran the blower, making a nice clean circle in the center of the floor and leaving a mountain of dirt around the sides.

Meanwhile, big sister got down on her hands and knees and began shoving toys under her bed. She pushed and she shoved until everything was crammed underneath. Then, she very carefully arranged the bedspread so that it hung down over the sides of the bed and hid the toys lurking below.

[Show the tower of toys and brother creating a pile of dust with a hand-held blower similar to a leaf blower. Show dirt piling up like a sand dune around the edge of a completely clean circle in the middle of the room, and big sister stuffing toys under the bed.]

**Page 7**

"I'm done and ready for dessert," shouted big brother.

"I'm finished, too," said big sister, "but baby Grump's side of the room is a total disaster."

When it came time to clean, big sister always drew a line down the center of the room and explained that she and baby Grump would each clean on their half of the line. There somehow always seemed to be more toys on baby Grump's side.

As Mama stood surveying the girls' room, a loud crashing noise came from brother's room. Even Papa put down the newsboard and came in a dash. Brother's tower of toys was no more.

"That's not cleaning," said Mama. "This time put the toys away neatly on the shelf."

"Big sister didn't clean either," said baby Grump. "She just shoved everything under the bed or on my side of the room." Sure enough, when Mama lifted the bedspread, there sat tons of junk.

Mama sent everyone back to cleaning and put Papa in charge of blowing out the rooms.

[Show Papa making dust clouds with the blower.]


## Page 8

When the day to pick Grandma and Grandpa up at the airport finally arrived, the house looked sort of neat and tidy, as long as you didn't look under sister's bed or inside brother's closet.

Mama packed a picnic lunch to eat on the way to Grumpity City. Everyone was dressed in their finest. Just as Mama was about to announce that it was time to get in the grumpmobile, she looked out the window.

"No!" screeched Mama, "you can't go to the airport with sand in your fur."

Papa scurried baby Grump in from the sandbox and off to the bathtub as Mama searched for another clean dress.

[Show baby Grump in the bathtub splashing water everywhere with Mama in front of the chest-of-drawers tossing clothes in every direction.]


## Page 9

Mama climbed in the driver's seat and yelled, "Let's go, we're late." Papa crawled in on the other side and promptly started his nap. Everyone fastened their seat belts, and baby Grump had a perfect view from her grumpmobile seat.

Everything was going fine, until a tiny voice from the back seat said, "Are we there yet?" The ride was downhill from that moment on.

[Show the children squabbling in the back seat, Papa still sleeping, and Mama with a mean determined look on her face as she drives faster.]


## Page 10

At the airport, the Grump's arrived just as Grandma and Grandpa's grumpplane was landing.

"There they are!" announced brother.

A loud noise made everyone turn toward the rear of the grumpplane just in time to see Grandma and Grandpa's suitcases slide off the conveyor belt and fly open.

Clothes of every description were tossed high in the air. Grandma shrieked as the beads from her pearl necklace went rolling over the runway.

One of Grandma's skirts looked like an umbrella drifting up to the clouds, socks, t-shirts, even a pair of Grandpa's overalls got caught up by the wind and snagged the wing of the plane. It took three people to chase down a runaway shampoo bottle, and the wrapped packages Grandma and Grandpa had brought for the children were a secret no more.

[Show plane arriving, Grandma and Grandpa at the top of the stairs waving. Show suitcases popping open, clothes flying everywhere. Have gifts with name tags for brother, sister, and baby Grump. Have shampoo bottle keep rolling past everyone's grasp.]

## Page 11

When the Grumps and Grandma and Grandpa finally arrived back at the yellow cave, Papa Grump simply carted the contents of the suitcases into the cave and stacked them in one big heaping pile.

"Well, at least you don't have to get unpacked," said brother, "The wind did it for you." Grandma didn't look pleased.

Over dinner, talk turned to sightseeing. Grandma didn't want to go to the Berry Farm, too many bugs. Grandpa said, "If you've seen one farm you've seen 'em all." Sister mentioned a picnic by the waterfall. "Never," screeched Mama, "The height of that waterfall makes me dizzy. Baby Sister suggested the beach. "No, you'll get burned to a crisp," bellowed Papa. Brother thought people might simply enjoy driving around in the grumpmobile all day. Everyone started talking at once, not waiting for their turn. In a few minutes everyone was shouting so loud that the cave was about to burst wide open from the noise. Mama finally whistled between her fingers for silence. The cave fell deathly quiet. All eyes were trained on Mama.

[Show strawberry patch with giant bugs shaking hands and greeting guests as they arrive.]

## Page 12

"We need a plan," said Mama in a whisper. Papa got out his whittling knife and a piece of bark to take notes. "Everyone" Mama said very softly, "will suggest one place that they would like to go and tell why that would be a fun trip for the entire family. We'll start with baby sister."

Baby sister still wanted to go to the beach. Big sister was dead set on the waterfall. Big brother just wanted to drive around in the grumpmobile. Grandma was sound asleep. Grandpa had swiped Papa's newsboard and only grunted when it came his turn. Papa shrugged his shoulders and said, "I don't care." Mama reminded Papa that there wasn't a place called "I don't care." He'd need to think of something else.

"There most certainly is a place called *I Don't Care*. It's down the other side of the valley," Papa beamed. "They serve *I Don't Care Burgers* and *I Don't Care Soda* under a big spreading *I Don't Care Tree*. There's even an *I Don't Care Children's Museum* to keep busy paws out of trouble," said Papa."

"Can we go? Can we go?"

"I don't care," snorted Grandpa as he flipped the newsboard over to read what was carved on the back.

"The vote's unanimous," cheered Papa with pride.

[Draw a picture of *I Don't Care*.]


**Page 13**

The next morning, Mama packed two brimming full picnic baskets for lunch. She didn't trust Papa's *I Don't Care Burgers*. She said he was probably making the whole thing up.

The Grumps drove deep into the valley, deeper than the children had ever been before.

Just as the children were about to give up hope of ever getting there, a banner stretched across the road read, "Welcome to *I Don't Care*, Population 3." Another sign next to a big hole in the middle of the road read, "Your City Taxes at Work."

[Show Papa driving underneath the sign and around a pothole larger than the car. Have a shovel and pile of dirt sitting beside the hole.]


**Page 14**

"All out," Papa bellowed, "for fun and *I Don't Care* excitement galore."

Inside the Children's Museum there was a water table where you could make mud pies. Baby sister splattered mud everywhere.

Big sister liked the doll house station. Mama helped sister make furniture out of tiny circles of cork. They made sofas, tables with chairs, beds, lamps, and even a refrigerator and stove for the kitchen. Grandma found a motorized rocking chair.

There was also a miniature grummobile on a track. Big brother spent the entire day driving around and around the museum. Grandpa and Papa took turns as back-seat drivers.

"No, go right! Now, left! Turn! Stop!" They could be heard shouting from every corner of the museum.

[Show baby sister in the mud, Grandma sleeping in the motorized rocking chair, and Mama and big sister gluing doll house furniture together. Show brother as a wild driver and Papa or Grandpa hanging on for dear life pointing and shouting in the other direction.]

**Page 15**

Papa bought *I Don't Care Burgers and Soda* for everyone. They sat underneath the *I Don't Care Tree* to eat. The drive back to the cave was peaceful. Everyone was pleasantly snoring, except for brother. Brother gripped an imaginary steering wheel as if he were still driving the grumpmobile. Mama barreled down the highway as always.

As they packed the sleepy children into the cave, Papa whispered, "Where to tomorrow?"

Mama replied with a smile, "I Don't Care."

[Have Mama and Papa carrying sleepy children off to bed and Grandpa tugging trying to wake up Grandma and get her out of the car.]

# Chapter 9
# Group Cohesion: The Therapeutic Factor in Groups

*He was a second grader still reading at the first grade level, a sweet little boy, described as being a behavior problem in the classroom. After observing him, I discovered that behavior wasn't the root cause of his problem. The little boy was very insecure and desperately wanted to fit in with the group. When he was paired with a student who worked on the assignment, he also studiously worked on the assignment. When he was placed with students who were being noisy and misbehaving, he too became noisy and disruptive. The student matched his behavior to fit the group with which he was placed. In essence, he wanted to belong and was willing to do whatever was needed to be accepted. When he was first placed in my after school program, I partnered him with studious participants so he would start off on a positive note. Slowly, I began challenging him to work independently. As he traveled from learning center to learning center, he began to feel more confident in his ability. As his self-efficacy improved, he no longer felt as desperate for acceptance. He then began to select others in the group with whom he wanted to interact. His behavior became more in keeping with his personality. He was no longer merely imitating what others were doing. As the group became more cohesive, he too became more confident and more willing to strike out on his own. On a free painting day, a day in which the students were allowed to paint anything they wanted without direction or assignment, the little boy looked at those gathered around the table but instead of imitating what others were painting, he began to paint his very own picture. He wasn't afraid to be different anymore. When others pointed out that he was painting something different from what they were painting, he simply smiled and continued. He felt accepted in the group and knew that it was acceptable to be different. A cohesive group that focused on rebuilding his self-efficacy enabled the little boy to return to the classroom and feel confident enough to project his own self-image.*

Group cohesion is the relationship among members in a group, but group cohesion is more than just a relationship (Yalom and Leszcz 2005). As shown in the opening example, sometimes students sacrifice everything just to be accepted by a group. Cohesion does not mean simply doing what someone else wants you to do or merely getting along with others. Group cohesion is a positive bond that exists between all group members. You cannot have group cohesion if one or more members of the group are ostracized or subdued into compliance. For group cohesion to be

Clanton Harpine, *Group-Centered Prevention Programs for At-Risk Students*,
DOI 10.1007/978-1-4419-7248-4_9, © Springer Science+Business Media, LLC 2011

positive and constructive, it must be part of a warm supportive group environment, empathic understanding and acceptance must be shared by all group participants, and there must be a strong sense of attachment or feeling of belonging among individual participants and the group. Group cohesion provides the bond within the group which helps group members heal old wounds of negativism and pursue new pathways of success. Therefore, your program must develop and maintain constructive, positive group cohesion.

## Paving the Way for Cohesion and Change

It is easy to say that a group must be cohesive, but helping a group become cohesive is a different matter. Let's look at an example from my 9-month *Reading Orienteering Club* program to illustrate the importance of group cohesion. I typically launch the 9-month program with the intensive week-long *Camp Sharigan* reading clinic. Interaction, cohesion, and motivation are usually strong during the first week because *Camp Sharigan* is fast-paced and exciting, but it is hard to maintain such fast-paced excitement over a 9-month period. Consequently, whereas discipline problems are rare during *Camp Sharigan*, problems do arise as students settle into the monthly pace of the *Reading Orienteering Club*.

An example of rebuilding cohesion arose with a *Reading Orienteering Club* group. The group was in the third month of a 9-month program. The newness had worn off and group members were returning to their typical classroom-style behavior: running down the hall (which had been forbidden many times), getting loud and boisterous at learning centers, pushing and shoving each other, grabbing glue and pencils from others, leaning back on two legs in their chairs. This type of behavior destroys cohesion and could turn a good program into disaster.

I interjected a new mascot or character into the program named *Ollie Octopus* (Clanton Harpine 2011). I wrote stories, developed craft projects, and created behavior problems which *Ollie* had to overcome. *Ollie* became the modeling example that the children were challenged to follow. As *Ollie* changed his behavior and became happier, illustrated through stories and activities, the group members also changed their behavior and became more cohesive. We made *Ollie Octopus* puppets, *Ollie Octopus* name tags, and *Ollie Octopus* pop-up books. *Ollie Octopus* became a make-believe friend who taught the children how to work together in a group.

The idea was to create a make-believe character that was experiencing the same feelings and having the same problems as the children in the group. As the children helped *Ollie* solve his problems, they began to find ways to change their behavior as well. Storytelling and puppets became therapeutic techniques which led to change: "What would Ollie do in this situation? Let's see if we can help Ollie out today. Remember, no jet propulsion down the hallway." Ollie became a fun corrective tool.

Cohesion does not simply occur when students are placed in a group. Cohesion must be built into your program design. Cohesion will not occur if your group is plagued with discipline problems, uncooperative group members, domineering personalities, reluctant uninvolved group members, or participants who feel shunned or ostracized. Each and every member of your group must feel accepted for group cohesion to exist, and your group must work together as a cohesive unit if your program is to be successful.

## Using Therapeutic Factors in Group Programming

If the program you are designing is to be cohesive, you must focus on the therapeutic power of group process. Irvin Yalom describes the underlying structure of group process which works to bring about change as the following 11 therapeutic factors: instillation of hope, universality, imparting information, altruism, recapitulation of the primary family group, development of socializing techniques, imitative behavior, interpersonal learning, group cohesiveness, catharsis, and existential factors (Yalom and Leszcz 2005). To develop a cohesive group program, those 11 factors must be built into your program design. Sometimes those factors work differently in a group-centered intervention than they do in psychotherapy, but the 11 factors are present just the same. Let's examine these factors in reference to how they work in a group-centered prevention program.

*Hope* is one of the basic elements of therapy; without hope, there cannot be healing. Without hope, there cannot be change. Hope is essential in psychologically based groups. The need to belong is fundamental for any age and in any group (Baumeister and Leary 1995). We want others to like us. We want to be included. In school, we must think that we can succeed, that we can learn, and that we can change when needed (Deci and Ryan 1985). Believing that we can change, learn, or improve is the first step to success. We must believe that something is possible before we will begin to work toward making a change. A positive cohesive atmosphere in a group sets the stage for this feeling of hope. Students must want to be involved in a group in order for it to help them learn or change. The first minute of the first day introduces students to your new group and often determines whether they will be willing to participate or not. First impressions really do count. For your group program design to be effective, you must build cohesion and a feeling of acceptance into your group, a way for the participants to measure their success in the group, and most of all, the belief that change is possible. Your program design must incorporate hope. Negative groups do not create hope. Groups riddled with rules do not convey hope. Lectures about bad behavior do not instill hope. Discipline must be maintained, but your group design must make your participants want to comply, rather than force them to comply. Hope is positive, not punishing.

A word of caution here, especially when working in the schools. Many schools have mistakenly adopted the philosophy that positive self-esteem building means not correcting behavior. Nothing could be further from the truth. Pretending to build self-esteem while ignoring inappropriate behavior creates nothing but disaster (Baumeister et al. 2003), and for self-esteem to be worthwhile, it must be real, not contrived. An example of inappropriate self-esteem building comes from an elementary school. A little boy was sent to the principal's office because of his inappropriate behavior in the classroom; the entire class saw the boy get in trouble and return to the classroom with candy and a sparkly pencil. What did the child learn? He learned how to be rewarded for misbehaving in the classroom. What did the remainder of the class learn? They learned that if you want candy and a sparkly pencil, you must misbehave in class. True self-esteem is only enhanced if the student learns that he is a special person because of who he is or something that he did. Bribes of candy do not improve self-esteem.

With the *Reading Orienteering Club* group mentioned earlier, group behavior had become rowdy and out-of-control. I did not give the students stickers or candy to make them feel better about themselves. I sat the misbehaving students down and we discussed their behavior and only the misbehaving students were included (never include students who are behaving in discussions of misbehavior). I informed the misbehaving group that their behavior was unacceptable. I reassured them that I cared deeply for them, but that their behavior would have to change. I discussed injuries that could occur from running in the hallway or leaning backward in a chair. I spelled out every single mistake they had made and explained very carefully what I expected them to do. I then came back in the next session and had *Ollie* try to control his behavior after getting in trouble in the ocean. I did not pretend that misbehaving was okay. I also knew that just telling the students that their behavior was unacceptable would not make them change. I reinforced the changes that I wanted the students to make through stories with *Ollie*. I continually reminded the students that as children they were fine; it was their behavior that had to change. Through stories and a puppet, I showed the children how to change their behavior and through the process, developed a stronger more cohesive group. The children did not receive candy or an award for changing their behavior; instead, I found a reason to compliment and praise every group member, even those who had not been in trouble. Change occurred as the group members began to work together and care about the group. Hope becomes one of the first and most essential elements for any group-centered intervention.

*Universality.* All students fear rejection. Feelings of rejection make the situation even worse, but learning that others are worried that they will not be accepted by the group, make a desired grade, or find a friend can sometimes lessen the fear of rejection. We are all individuals but we also share similarities. Learning that others have the same fears, problems, likes, and dislikes can be the first step to bringing a group closer together. Group structure makes commonality and the act of accepting others more likely.

At one test site for the *Camp Sharigan* program, individual interviews were conducted with students preceding and following the week-long reading camp (Clanton Harpine 2005a). At that site, students were selected for the program because of failing grades in reading. One little boy remarked that he was certain that he was the only student in his class that could not read. Then, when he arrived at the camp, there were four other students from his class at *Camp Sharigan*. He was shocked to discover that he was not the only student still having trouble in reading. At the follow-up interview, he promised that he was going to work with his new "friends," just the way *Sharigan* had taught during the camp. "When we get back to class, we're going to be a team," the little boy said, "just like at *Camp Sharigan.*"

Your program can become the catalyst for change not only during the program but after the program as well. Your program design must help participants see that they are not the only ones struggling in the classroom. Combine the feeling of hope with the sense that "no one is an island."

Like the teens in the opening example in Chapter 2, the group setting helped the teenagers to realize that they were not the only ones needing help. They were a group and everyone in the group was working on improving their reading skills. There is comfort in being an accepted member of a group.

*Imparting Information.* All groups *impart information*, but the manner in which groups teach or inform can make the difference between success and failure. On the one hand, psychoeducational groups often use direct instruction from the group leader. On the other hand, group-centered interventions use learning centers, hands-on activities, and even community service to teach and inform. The learning center task may be focused on reading comprehension or phonics while simultaneously teaching group skills and how to work together as a group. Students go to the learning center, work on skill building activities, and learn to work with others in the process. Skill-building is a vital step in rebuilding self-efficacy and is an essential ingredient of every group-centered intervention. With group-centered interventions, students become active seekers of knowledge and skills and are active participants in the learning process.

At *Camp Sharigan*, learning centers teach spelling, reading, comprehension, writing, phonics, new methods for learning *tricky words*, and how to read and follow directions. Puppet plays help children improve fluency, reading intonation, and listening skills. Information is shared through the learning center instructions. Students learn new skills through hands-on application of the information they obtain from each learning center. The learning center activity becomes the avenue through which students learn, instead of worksheets or lectures as frequently used in the classroom. Sometimes the learning center is focused on teaching individual skill-building activities (phonics, oral reading, or writing a story using correct grammatical sentence structure). Other times, the learning center may be focused on building group skills. Group tasks such as painting a puppet stage teach students how to work together as a group and in the classroom.

Children love to paint. At *Camp Sharigan* the children are given a large piece of cloth, usually an old bed sheet (my programs all emphasize using recyclable materials), a tablecloth, or leftover fabric (Clanton Harpine 2010a). As they arrive at the learning center, the children are instructed to paint a puppet stage as a group. There are typically 30 children at *Camp Sharigan*. Therefore, the children are told to start at the top and work their way to the bottom of the cloth. The children are allowed to paint whatever they would like, as long as it is positive and they make sure that everyone is included and has a place to paint. Children must organize the painting so that everyone can be included, and then, as new children come to the learning center, they must add on to what has already been painted. In this way, painting a puppet stage becomes a group project which requires 30 children to work together to paint one piece of cloth. Information is shared and group skills are taught as the children work together.

*Altruism.* Any time we allow students to give or act kindly to others, it helps the individual student and also helps to build a stronger sense of group cohesion. All too often children perceive themselves to just be receivers. They wait to see what someone will give them, and they expect all gifts to be for them. Giving is therapeutic. Helping someone else is therapeutic. Building teamwork, sharing kindness, or finding a way for participants to help others strengthens the goals you wish to achieve in your program.

One of my after school groups planned a party. We baked cookies and, naturally, sampled several. We also packaged and sent extra cookies to a local nursing home. One little boy remarked, "Why are we giving them our cookies? Why don't we just take the extra cookies home?" This opened the door for a discussion of how the residents would feel when we delivered our freshly baked cookies to them for dinner. "The little boy then said, "They're going to be happy because these are good cookies." All too often we wait to see what we will be given without ever thinking what we can give. Learning to give kindly to others is an essential ingredient for healthy group structure because in a group, members must think of the needs of those around them. Group members cannot just be concerned with what they want; they must also be concerned with the quiet, shy member who doesn't speak or with the group member who is always acting out seeking attention.

I incorporate service to others into children's programs as well as programs for teenagers. Sometimes service to others is incorporated into the group itself, but often, it is directed toward the community and those in need. The puppet play intervention presented at the end of this chapter is a perfect example of how skill building (vocabulary building and learning to read new and difficult words) and community service can be combined. Teens and older elementary students can work in class or in an after school program to practice and prepare the puppet play. Then, they can travel to an elementary school or local nursing home to share their presentation. Giving to others becomes an important component of group process. Community service projects help students begin to think of the needs and feelings of others so that they can then apply these same skills to the members of their group.

*Group.* The *classroom group* or *peer group* is recreated in the new group that you form. Your group becomes the therapy group. If your group is accepting and positive, then students begin to think that change is possible. Your group then becomes the laboratory in which students learn new skills and become better able to handle classroom problems which caused them to fail. Your school-based prevention group can teach children and teens new ways of behaving, working together, and learning. Your group also becomes a new peer group, especially with teens.

*Camp Sharigan* helps the children become a close knit group. After working together for five straight days, 2 hours a day, children and workers alike feel a closeness, a desire to work together, a desire to help each other. This closeness is the foundation for therapeutic change.

For your program design, be sure to build in ways for the members to work together to solve problems, to complete an activity, or to accomplish a task. Working together as equal members of a team infuses hope, acceptance, and support into every facet of your program.

*Social skills.* Changing social behavior is often one of the primary roles of school counselors. The program you design can become a real world experience in which group members can work on problems and projects that may require learning specific new skills. Group interaction and working in a cohesive group allows group members to see the impact of their behavior on others in the group. This can be especially important with teenage groups and groups working on classroom behavior. By working together in a group setting, group participants can learn new ways to solve old problems. Group members can also practice being less judgmental, rude, argumentative, or bullying. Group programs provide a safe place for students to practice skills.

Academic failure often goes hand-in-hand with experiencing problems with social skills in the classroom. One example comes from a sixth grader who had once been retained in school and was still struggling in reading. This young man was placed in a special behavioral class because of aggressive behavior in the classroom. After working in one of my after school programs over the course of 4 or 5 months, the young man was allowed to return to the regular classroom. Once his remedial reading problems were corrected, his anger and aggression melted away. In my after school group program, he had corrected his reading problems and practiced new ways to handle frustration so that when he returned to the classroom he would not lash out in anger when confronting new learning tasks or teasing from others. The after school program became a safe group in which to experiment with acceptable behavior and responses. Make sure that your program design creates a safe group experience for practicing social skills and allows participants to explore new ways of responding to old problems.

Group-centered interventions use group process to create safe learning environments in which children and adolescents can experiment and learn new social skills and ways to interact with others in a group setting. Remember to build a social skills component into your group program design.

*Modeling.* Imitative behavior can be contagious, just as misbehaving can start with one student and soon consume an entire class, modeling correct behavior can also spread through an entire group. Modeling is particularly effective with students diagnosed with attention deficit hyperactivity disorder (ADHD). Where direct instruction and one-on-one tutoring often fail to bring about change in classroom behavior with students diagnosed with ADHD, group-centered interventions which allow all students to practice desired behavior frequently succeed.

Again, I used painting with a group. Children love to paint and rarely have an opportunity to do so at school; therefore, they are eager and motivated to cooperate in order to have an opportunity to paint. On this occasion, I structured the painting activity. Again, we were painting a puppet stage on cloth. Because children diagnosed with ADHD often have trouble controlling impulsive behavior, I had everyone sit around a large cluster of tables. The painting was placed in the center of the table. The children painted one at a time waiting patiently for a turn. Everyone was allowed to paint; no one was left out, but the order in which the children painted was determined by how well they modeled the desired behavior of sitting quietly in a chair and waiting for a turn. No reprimands were given, but positive praise was given to each child as they were called forward to paint: "Sally, why don't you come up and paint next because I see how patiently you are waiting." Even the most fidgety of students soon learned to sit quietly for a turn to paint.

The lesson did not end there. Next, as the students came forward to paint, each student was given a specific assignment, such as, "Sally, would you please paint six blades of grass here in this corner along the bottom of our cloth." Each assignment was very specific and controlled. Children received several opportunities to paint during the session but always in the same controlled manner. "Sally, would you please paint five trees here on the mountain." Each painting skill, such as painting grass or how to paint a tree, was demonstrated to each child in turn. Skill was not a consideration; these were easy tasks. The objective was to model control for a group project. The result was a wonderful puppet stage painted by the children, and they were very proud of their work. If I had instructed this group of children to design and paint their own puppet stage, it would have been a disaster because most of the group had been diagnosed with ADHD and were enrolled in my program because of lack of control in classroom settings. If allowed, they would get up and run around the room; they could not sit down in a chair correctly for even 5 seconds and they were always grabbing and fighting over supplies. The idea of taking turns was foreign to this group when we started. They were not ready to exhibit control. They first needed to learn control, and then, through modeling in a group setting, exhibit and practice that control during a fun hands-on group project. The success of the finished product is essential to the lesson of exhibiting control; therefore, choose a project that you are certain everyone can do successfullzzzy and that will look nice when completed. You want the students to be proud of what they accomplish.

*Interpersonal learning.* The program that you are organizing can serve as a reflective mirror through which group participants may see their actions and also the reactions of others in the group to their behavior. We learn through our interactions with others. If your group design does not incorporate group interaction, your group members will not have the opportunity to learn about interpersonal relationships. We do not learn how to interact with others through direct instruction, watching role plays, or viewing a movie. If you want to teach students how to interact with others in a group setting, you must place students in a group setting and create interactive situations or activities. Group interaction involves every member of the group, not just a chosen few to demonstrate how it should be done. Interpersonal learning takes place only when the group is totally interactive.

It goes without saying that such interaction must be positive, constructive, and cohesive. While some group therapy techniques do use a more confrontational style, group-centered interventions do not. Group-centered interventions stress change to bring about mental wellness and to enhance learning. If you wish to enhance learning, you can only do so in a positive motivational environment.

My previous example of a controlled painting exercise with children diagnosed with ADHD illustrates this point. If I had reprimanded students for not sitting quietly and waiting patiently for their turn, or if I had used a form of punishment, such as forfeiting a turn each time you're not sitting quietly, then students would have missed out on the modeling experience. If my tone was negative, their response would have been negative. Again, this does not mean that I believe misbehavior should go uncorrected. There should be classroom or group rules and students must be encouraged to follow them. At the same time, the way in which I lead students to follow class rules may well determine the level of interpersonal learning that takes place in my group. For example, a teacher wrote seven rules on the board: listen quietly when others are talking, take turns, don't lean your chair back on two legs.... The same general rules that I use in my own programs. Her enforcement was to have students stand up and read the rule they broke in front of the class. Students learned embarrassment, and possibly compliance, but not eager acceptance. Students did not comply in this classroom situation because they wanted to; the teacher's method was not intrinsic. Students complied because of fear or embarrassment. What did students learn? They learned resentment, anger, and frustration. For interpersonal learning to take place, there must be a positive, constructive component in the experience.

Therefore, in your program design, think of positive ways to help students learn the rules. Lead and guide students toward compliance rather than through coercion or bribery. Students will actually learn more if they learn how to change their behavior in a cohesively supportive group rather than just learning to comply with the rules to keep from getting in trouble. The group structure is a perfect place in which to learn classroom management.

*Group cohesiveness.* Cohesion unites group members with common ties of friendship, acceptance, and belonging. Cohesion must be positive. In order for cohesion to be positive in a group, all participants must feel that they are being treated and accepted equally. The stronger the cohesive bond between members of the group, the stronger the potential for permanent change. All group-centered interventions must incorporate cohesion.

One way in which I enhance cohesion in the *Camp Sharigan* program is through emphasis on teamwork. Throughout the week, I talk about the importance of teamwork. Through stories, puppet plays, working with a partner in the snake pit, and even through learning to share and take turns, cohesion and teamwork are stressed.

*Catharsis.* Group interaction lays the groundwork and provides the perfect setting for group members to express both positive and negative opinions, but catharsis, the freedom to express your feelings, can only be constructive if a strong cohesive bond has been established with the group. Honesty is essential for catharsis to take place, but you must make sure that when feelings are shared the group is ready to protect and honor each individual's feelings.

A graduate student of mine was leading a group in which a young fourth grader disclosed that he still cried when he was upset. After the group session, two members of the group started teasing and telling others in the class what the disclosing student had said. Naturally, a fight occurred. When the disclosing student was asked why he started the fight, he said, "I had to show I wasn't a cry baby."

Cohesion must be strong in a group for an open exchange of feelings to exist and to protect such an exchange of feelings when it occurs. Do not ask students to disclose personal information until you have built a strong cohesive bond between all group members. Catharsis is not just the sharing of personal feelings and information, it is caring enough about another person to understand how that person feels and to want to safeguard their feelings. If we have a strong cohesive bond, I do not want you to be embarrassed or to suffer from information that you might share in the group. If you are conducting a short-term group intervention, there may not be time in a 1-hour session, a 1-week or even a month-long program for such a cohesive bond to develop. Make sure that your group is truly ready before asking children and teens to disclose personal information that could be embarrassing or cause them pain. Catharsis is a process of healing; such healing will not occur if the student is further injured in the process.

*Existential factors.* Yalom's eleventh category, existential factors, implies accepting responsibility. Learning to accept responsibility is a major step in life. Life may be unfair even for children and teens. Poor health, family circumstances, parental problems, disabilities, and bad decisions may complicate the life of the student who joins your group. At some point, we must all accept the fact that we, and we alone, are responsible for the way in which we live and how we react to the situations and circumstances that we encounter. As long as students are looking for scapegoats, they are not ready to accept responsibility. Your task must be to get students beyond blaming others, beyond finding excuses, beyond giving up. Your task must be to enable the student to return to the class, face the situations and circumstances they find confronting them in the classroom, and still be successful. Unless the students are ready to accept that they are in control of their future and that they are responsible for the progress and success that they achieve, then they will never succeed.

Learning in a group environment is one of the best ways for students to move beyond anger and self-pity and achieve acceptance as they develop their own individual plan for success. The group program that you are designing may provide the perfect medium for learning to accept responsibility.

The 11 therapeutic factors presented by Yalom provide a structure upon which we can develop and design effective prevention groups. If we incorporate each of these factors in our group-centered prevention programs, we will be utilizing group process to its fullest extent. Not until we make full use of group process will we achieve success in group programming.

## Step 9: Building Therapeutic Factors into Your Program Design

How will you instill a sense of hope into your group design?

How will you create an atmosphere of acceptance and a feeling of universality among all group members?

What information will you teach through your program?

How will you prevent competition and build a group based on cooperation and altruistic attitudes toward others?

What kind of classroom structure will you build into your program?

How will you make sure that your group is a safe setting for practicing social group skills?

Does your group design offer opportunities for positive modeling of desired behavior?

How will you teach group members interpersonal skills and group interaction techniques?

What will you do to foster positive group cohesion?

How will you help students change and have a feeling of cathartic healing?

How will your group program teach students to have a sense of responsibility?

## Step 9, Design Example

*Hope.* A positive atmosphere generates a sense of hope from beginning to end at *Camp Sharigan.* I emphasize hope on an individual level by building in ways to show success. The *grapevine reading list* allows children to see improvement each day at the reading clinic. The reading lists are graded from easy to difficult and use vowel clustering. Children go to the grapevine each day at *Camp Sharigan* to capture five tricky words. Reading down the list until you capture five words actually means read down the paper strip until you find five words that you do not know, but instead we call it *capturing tricky words.* Learning new words becomes a game. A little boy was struggling one day at the *grapevine.* He had captured two words but seemed to be losing interest. When I stopped by his station, I asked, "How many words do you have?" He replied, "Only two." "Two's a good number," I said. "Why don't you go ahead and put your words up on the poison ivy vine." "No, I can find one more," he said eagerly. "Well, if you want to," I said with a smile. Looking for words that he did not know how to read had become a game. Once the little boy captured three words, he embarked upon the *4-step process* for learning the three words. The little boy knew this; therefore, he had actually volunteered to work harder than required.

*Universality.* Even though *Camp Sharigan* is for children in first through third grade, the program uses no designations of first, second, or third grade. *Camp Sharigan* instead uses a step system. Everyone starts at step one and then progresses up toward step four. No one is labeled by a step; everyone starts at step one each day. The steps are different each time, and the pace at *Camp Sharigan* is too brisk for anyone to keep track of how far someone read, thus alleviating competition. *Camp Sharigan* emphasizes reading, spelling, writing, and phonics. The children are often asked to write the ending for a story or to be a puppeteer and read for the puppet play. Each station emphasizes the skills needed to be an effective reader.

*Altruism. Camp Sharigan* has the children work in teams (in small groups) to help each other. The theme for the week is working together as a team. Sometimes, I also incorporate a service project, such as presenting the Friday puppet show to a younger group of children, to parents, or for the community if we are at a community center.

*Classroom group. Camp Sharigan* stresses problem solving and critical thinking. The children must learn to follow step-by-step directions in order to complete a project. *Camp Sharigan* also teaches children to be actively involved in the learning process through hands-on activities at the learning centers. There are no lectures and no workbooks. *Camp Sharigan* is totally hands-on and active from the minute the children arrive until they leave.

*Social skills.* Children at *Camp Sharigan* practice social skills through learning to interact and work together as a group. Puppet plays are an excellent way to teach cooperation. Painting the puppet stage requires that each participant think about the needs and feelings of the other students in the group before painting. Students cannot just paint whatever they want; they must work together with 30 other students and compromise. The puppet stage provides an excellent lesson in social skills.

*Modeling.* Movement and interaction provide opportunities for modeling at *Camp Sharigan.* Students see other students moving around the room from station to station, working, completing projects, and making sure that they go to all 10 stations on their *treasure hunt map.* One parent explained, "I have so much trouble getting him to read. He comes here, follows his map, and reads every station sign, story, and book that you put before him. Why won't he read for me?" The answer was modeling. The little boy saw others reading and working, and so he was motivated to do the same.

*Interpersonal learning.* The individual one-on-one tutoring interaction between *camp guides* and participating students at *Camp Sharigan* provides a perfect arena for children to learn not only reading skills, but also to learn about their approach to learning. One student explained, "At school I always get in trouble. The teacher always yells at me to focus." The student had been diagnosed with ADHD, and I was a little worried that the constant movement from station to station and noise level might have been bothering the student. However, she said, "No, and there's always someone to help you when you get stuck on a word." Incorporating one-on-one tutoring in a group setting provides a whole new approach to learning.

*Group cohesiveness.* The group is essential to the effectiveness of *Camp Sharigan.* The students look forward to coming each day and build their own sense of community through working together during the week. Every aspect of *Camp Sharigan,* from action stories which allow children to act out parts of the story as it is being told, to puppet plays, stresses group cohesion. Group cohesion is an essential ingredient in any effective group-centered prevention program.

*Catharsis. Camp Sharigan* does not involve therapeutic disclosure, but it does provide catharsis and healing through the rebuilding of self-efficacy. By teaching children the skills they need to be successful in reading and by rebuilding their confidence and belief in themselves, *Camp Sharigan* helps children return to the classroom ready to learn.

*Responsibility.* First, *Camp Sharigan* teaches children that they can succeed. Then, it provides the motivation to return to the classroom and accept the responsibility for learning. Once children believe they can do a job; they are more motivated to try.

# Real-World Applications

## *Observational Extensions*

Observe the students you wish to include in your new group, do you notice any particular needs or problems? Sometimes students will need help outside of the group structure. Be alert to students who may need special assistance.

## *Troubleshooting Checklists for Designing a New Group-Centered Program*

1. Does anything about your program proposal trouble you?
2. Are there any safety issues? Safety means both physical and psychological.
3. How will you fix these programming problems?
4. If you cannot completely fix a problem, how will you reduce or work around the problem?

## *A Ready-to-Use Group-Centered Intervention: "The World Pollution Conference Puppet Play"*

**Age level:** This is an excellent intervention for older elementary, middle school, and high school students.
**Learning Objective:** To develop and strengthen vocabulary skills and phonological skills.
**Counseling Objective:** To enhance group cohesion and to teach group skills through teamwork.
**Time needed:** 1 week or 5 hours

*Tips for Using this Group-Centered Intervention*: This group-centered intervention works well with older students who need to work on phonics. The pollution theme brings forth words that the students would not typically know; therefore, students must use phonics skills and dictionary skills to learn to pronounce these new words but there is no shame in not knowing or practicing the pronunciation of such words.

*How to Expand into a Group-Centered Prevention Program*: You can simply have students read the puppet play or you can expand this intervention by allowing the students to present the puppet play to possibly a younger group of children. The group might make a puppet stage by painting a piece of cloth, make puppets from recyclable materials, and then practice and present the play. Such a group project emphasizes teamwork and is an excellent way to build group cohesion. The puppet play is presented in four parts to make it easier to work on in a week-long session. This group-centered intervention is an excellent illustration of how to expand and develop programming ideas into week-long experiences which both teach and contribute to personal growth and well-being.

*Supplies needed*: A copy of the script for each student, cloth for a puppet stage (cloth is better than paper and you can even use an old bed sheet or tablecloth), paint brushes, tempera paint for the puppet stage, recyclable materials for puppets (cereal boxes, plastic bottles, buttons, tissue rolls, bits of yarn, stuffing from old pillows – any recyclable object will work), glue, construction paper scraps, scissors, pencils, crayons or markers, hole punch, and a small bottle of bubbles for the play.

## List of Puppets

If you would like to make puppets, the following descriptions can be used to give students helpful hints. The puppets are arranged in order to when they appear in the play.

*Needed for Monday*

1. Reporter (give him a hat – write *Save the Whales and Be Kind to Dolphins* on puppet's hat and shirt)
2. Committee – three people who sit behind a desk or table (use paper plate puppets and place them behind a desk or table – should be all one piece)
3. Dust – need six dust balls (use round circles, gray, brown, and black paper – add stuffing color with markers or spray paint with tempera if possible – put on black elastic so that they bounce)
4. Soot – (make twin smoke stacks and a car with black smoke coming out – need three of each, make sure each has black smoke coming out)
5. Grime – (shiny new car that flips around and is covered in splotches of black, gray grime – may have two or three)
6. Picket Signs: *Freedom* signs and *Don't Pollute* signs

*Needed for Tuesday*

7. Carbon Monoxide – (invisible, reading part only – use the bubbles for the play)
8. Toxic chemicals (benzene, xylene, and toluene) – (for these chemicals make a big gas truck delivering gas to a gas station – may have one or two of each – also for make-believe chemicals for the play make round blue circles, decorate with eyes, noses, sunglasses, caps, whatever, cover with blue cotton balls)
9. Toxic chemicals found in houses, apartment buildings, stores, and factories – make one of each – extras are fine here

*Needed for Wednesday*

10. Sulfur (a yellow cloud – use yellow confetti for acid rain)

11. White puffy clouds that turn gray on the other side – (need lots of gray clouds – as many as eight – clouds may be dressed up with sunglasses, hats, fancy long eyelashes, etc.)
12. Nitrogen oxide – airplanes and diesel trucks and buses – one of each (make paper airplanes that fly over edge of puppet stage – have about six airplanes)
13. Sunshine – (only one – use paper curls for rays and cotton balls for fuzzy effect)
14. Smog – one long gray that covers everything – (try to find a sheer gray scrap of fabric that can be unrolled)
15. Ozone – (make a girl puppet with holes in her dress)
16. Foam cups and foam packing pellets- nothing to make (just collect)
17. Carbon dioxide – (make trees for the forest, trees will be cut down and burned to let off carbon dioxide – make about 12 trees and 6 fires – tree puppets will have two handles, one for upright, and two for lying down – fires are made out of red, orange, and yellow tissue and rolled paper for logs)
18. You want to have both good and bad pollution signs – the good signs will chase away the bad signs by the end of the play: children may also make "tasteful" picket signs, such as (1) Keep the air dirty vote for me, (2) Keep asbestos floating in the sky; tear down old buildings; and set me free, (3) Keep the air polluted, drive your car everyday or good signs, (1) Don't pollute, (2) Care about the world around you, (3) Save the Earth.

## Play

*The World Pollution Conference*

*Have gray clouds overhead and the sun barely visible from behind the gray clouds. Start the play with picket signs waving everywhere and shouts and chants being heard by the audience. Then have reporter appear.*

## Part I

First Picketer:    Dust and grime; we're not a crime. (Shouted loudly three times, then whispered in background.)

Second Picketer: Freedom; freedom; we want freedom; freedom; freedom; give us freedom; let us pollute. (Chanted loudly at first and then whispered in background.)

Third Picketer:   Down with the ozone; no more ozone. (Shouted like a cheer. Said only once, not repeated.)

Reporter:         Welcome, on this glorious, sunny summer day. (Reporter puppet looks around.) There's a sun out here somewhere. You have to be careful though; it's getting dangerous to breathe. (cough) We have so many chemicals floating around here today as we report live, downtown from the World Pollution Conference that we may need to start passing out gas masks soon. (several people cough) We'll be going inside the conference center in just a moment where each nasty pollution-causing agent will testify before the panel and explain why they should be allowed to remain in the air, water, or soil. As the competition heats up, it will be interesting to see who survives and who gets terminated. (coughs again) Come on, let's go inside; this fresh outdoor air is killing me.

(Everyone moves inside the convention center. Picketers March carrying signs in front of committee. Reporter and Dusty enter the scene.)

Dust Picketers:  Dusty, Dusty, we want Dusty (picketers wave signs saying, Keep Dusty, Long Live Dusty).

Dusty:  Madame President, I am here to say that having dust in your house, in your car, flying out of the backs of dump trucks, and at each and every farm across the nation is not what blackens the skies. It's soot and grime that are doing all the damage not me. You shouldn't get rid of me. Yes, sometimes I know it's hard to breathe when the air's full of dirt, but that's not my fault. People should be at work not outside enjoying a late afternoon walk. There's no such thing as fresh air anymore.

Committee #1:  That's what we're here trying to fix, Dusty. We want clean air, fresh water, and safe soil and we intend to get rid of anything and every-thing that stands in our way, including you. (a rousing cheer of *Clean air, clean air, give us clean, clean air* starts up from the other end of the puppet stage complete with clean air signs) You, dear Dusty, go on the termination list unless someone worse comes along (the gavel pounds).

Dusty:  That's not fair, what's a little dirt going to hurt? You should talk to Mr. Soot over there. He's much worse than I am.

Soot:  Hey Dusty, don't take it out on me just because they didn't want you. Not everyone can be as wonderful as I am.

Committee #1:  Wonderful! What do you call each and every car, truck, and bus on the road? What about smoke stacks (use black confetti for smoke-stack pollution), power plants, wood burning stoves, backyard barbecues, brush piles, factories....

Soot:  Uh, well, uh, that's just the cost of doing business and having fun.

Committee #1:  It's a cost we can do without. You go on the termination list too.

Soot:  Hey, that's not fair. There are a lot of guys out there worse than I am.

Committee #2:  Name one please, Mr. Soot.

Soot:  What about Grimey?

Committee #3:  Excellent idea! Let's get rid of Grime too.

Grimey:  Not me, I haven't done anything. I never hang out with those guys. You're mistaken. We're not friends.

| | |
|---|---|
| Dusty: | Come on, give us another chance. |
| Soot: | You're not being fair. |
| Grimey: | Wait till you see who's coming next. |
| | (Dust, Soot, and Grime are hauled away as bubbles start floating up from behind stage. House and apartment puppets appear.) |

## Part II

| | |
|---|---|
| Committee #1: | Carbo, is that you blowing bubbles? |
| Carbon Monoxide: | Do you see me blowing bubbles? (spoken in a low voice) |
| Committee #1: | Very funny. You like to sneak up on people, don't you? |
| Carbon Monoxide: | That's me, Carbon Monoxide, the sneakiest fellow in town. You can't see me. You can't touch me. You can't feel me, but I'm here. Do you have a headache? Do you feel tired, lifeless? (gives a mean, nasty laugh) It could be me (loud yawning is heard) getting sleeping, thought so (release a partially blown up balloon) oops, your dead! |
| Committee #1: | (yawns big and loud) You definitely go on the list, Carbo. Get out of here. |
| Benzene: | And good riddance too. I'm sure glad you're clearing those guys out; they are bad news, man. They're not nice like us. |
| Committee #1: | And you are? |
| Benzene: | We're Benzene, Xylene, and Toluene. |
| Xylene: | We don't make your eyes itch like Dusty. |
| Toluene: | Or make your throat hurt from breathing in Soot. |
| Xylene: | We don't get into the water like Grimey. |
| Benezene: | And we don't make you sleepy the way Carbo does. |
| Committee #2: | Aren't you guys poisonous? |
| Benezene: | Oh well, yeah, you could say that. We're found in gasoline, asbestos, mercury, and lead. We particularly love old buildings with asbestos ceilings that crumble and float down like little tiny snowflakes (throw white confetti). And do you have any idea how many cars and truks there are on the road? |
| Reporter: | 35 million at last count |
| Xylene: | And they burn over 200 billion gallons of gasoline which fills the air with US. |
| Toluene: | Every single car and truck that drives down the road is spewing out benzene and me, and do I love it when people work so hard to send me spewing out of tailpipes all around the world. Let's see, I've been to London, Paris, China, Japan, Australia… |
| Picketers: | (chants) Cars and trucks, cars and trucks, come on people we need more….cars and trucks. |
| Benzene: | We don't make you sneeze like dust, soot, and grime. We just… |

Committee #1:    ...cause cancer, lung disease, and kill people.
Benzene:         You can't prove that. That study's biased. It's also not true what they say about us getting into the water and contributing to acid rain.
Committee #1:    Enough, out of here, we're tired of you and your kind. We're cleaning up the air and the water. We're going to find ways to get rid of you. (Sulfy enters as Committee talks)


**Part III**

Sulfy:           (laughs) I told you guys that you didn't stand a chance.
Committee #1:    And who might you be?
Sulfy:           Sulfur Dioxide at your service, ma'am, but my friends just call me Sulfy. Smokestacks (throw black confetti) are my specialty, power plants, coal, that sort of thing, but I do my best work in the rain. (whistles a tune)
Committee #3:    And why is that?
Sulfy:           I get into the air and mix with the moisture in the clouds. Then I come down as rain, acid rain to be exact. (throw yellow confetti over top of puppet stage)
Committee #1:    Doesn't acid rain kill trees and fish?
Sulfy:           Well...
Committee #1:    And what about the statues and buildings?
Sulfy:           I know, wasn't that funny how I took that statue's nose right off his face? (laughs)
Committee #1:    No!
Sulfy:           I sometimes have to travel for hundreds of miles to do my dirty work. You can't get rid of me; I actually work hard to make it difficult for people to breathe. And besides, I'm not nearly as bad as those other guys.
Oxi:             He's right, you know. He's not nearly as bad as me.
Committee #1:    And you are?
Oxi:             I am Nitrogen Oxide or Oxi for short. And I can do twice the damage of Sulfy. Every time a car, plane, truck, bus, factory, or power plant burns fuel, any fuel, I'm there. I make your lungs hurt and make it hard for you to breathe. I get into the water like Sulfy does and make acid rain, but here's the good part, the part Sulfy can't do, I make smog. (uncurl gray sheer cloth over the top of the puppet stage) That's right, when the cars and trucks barrel down the highway pouring nitrogen oxide out their tail pipes and the sun beats down and warms me up, I go to work and make life miserable for everyone. I burn your eyes, make your lungs feel tight, your head ache. There's no one who can hold a candle to me. I am the best.

| Reporter: | You're the best all right; you're the best at killing animals. You get into lakes, streams, rivers, ponds, even the ocean, and you eventually seep into the water supply. You kill everything you come in contact with. |
| Ozone: | (comes out sniffing and pretending to cry) And look what he did to my dress! Oxi and his friends poked holes into the ozone layer of my dress and ruined it. It will never be the same (cries loudly). |
| CFC Dudes: | (have CFC trio enter doing a little chant – *We are the CFCs; we are the best you see; no one's better than CFC; we are the CFCs*). |
| CFC #1: | We come to you straight from plastic (throw a plastic bag over top of stage), foam (toss a foam cup), fast food, packing pellets (throw several handfuls of packing pellets), refrigerators, air conditioners (make refrigerator and air conditioner paper puppets to hold up); we've got it all. |
| Committee #1: | Did you poke holes in the ozone layer? |
| CFC #1: | Sure, why not; and besides, holes let in radiation. |
| CFC #2: | And don't try to blame it all on us. Who stopped at the fast food drive-in yesterday – yep, we saw you with those waxed paper products, Styrofoam, and plastic. |
| CFC #3: | Or let the coolant leak out of your air conditioner or refrigerator. Don't bother with repairs or to recycle; just throw the thing away. It's easy, no sweat. |
| CFC #1: | There's also aerosol spray cans for hair spray, paint; you name it, if it's in an aerosol can, you've got CFCs. Trust me, everybody's doing it. I mean, who needs an ozone layer anyway? I sure don't. |
| Committee: | Well, we do. We can't live without the ozone layer. So we're getting rid of all of you, Sulfy, Oxi, and, you, CFC Dudes. You're history, terminated. |
| CFC #1: | Hey, that's not fair. It's not our fault that you cut down so many trees, built so many power plants, burn gasoline, diesel fuel, and coal. We weren't the ones that told you to use foam and plastic because you were too lazy to wash dishes. |
| Committee #1: | You're right CFC, and we're going to change. First stop, my house. Look around the garage, do you have motor oil, gasoline for the lawn mower, paint cans, fertilizer, pesticides for the garden? |
| Committee #2: | Do you sweep grass clippings and leaves into the street to be washed down the storm drain and into the water supply? |
| Committee #1: | Do you buy aerosols because they are more convenient and spray better than pump sprays? Do you recycle? |
| Reporter: | They say that a good measure of how well you're doing in the fight to Recycle, Reuse, and Reduce is that if you put your trash and recycling out on the same day, side by side, you should have three times as much recycling as you do trash? |
| Committee #3: | Three times as much! |

| | |
|---|---|
| Reporter: | That's right. Garbage is one of our biggest pollution problems. (throw waded up pieces of paper, more Styrofoam, paper cups, plates, plastic containers) The latest report estimates that we generate five billion tons of garbage a year and about 15% of that is hazardous, that breaks down to approximately four pounds of trash per person every single day, no wonder our landfills are busting at the seams. They say that we throw away enough iron and steel to build every new car coming off the assembly line this year and that we throw away more than enough aluminum drink cans to more than rebuild every single commercial airplane now flying every 3 months. |
| Committee #2: | You mean, we could have a new airplane every 3 months? |
| Reporter: | That's right. And here's the bad part, we throw away enough recyclable paper, not counting newspaper, like envelopes from the mail, office paper, school papers, computer paper, to build a wall of paper 12 feet high from New York City to Los Angeles. If we could stack all of the bottles, jars, and cans that are thrown into the trash, we'd be able to build a tower taller than the highest skyscraper every month. |

## Part IV

| | |
|---|---|
| Committee #1: | Every time you wash your car in the driveway, grime and detergent pour down the driveway and into the storm drain and straight to your water supply. |
| Committee #2: | Every quart of motor oil, new or used, pollutes thousands of gallons of drinking water and kills hundreds of animals. |
| Reporter: | They even found a 50-year-old carrot and a hot dog in a landfill that were still totally intact. There wasn't enough oxygen in the landfill to allow the carrot and hot dog to decompose. |
| Committee #3: | That's awful. What can we do? |
| Reporter: | Change the way we live. (have picketers put down pollution signs and pick up save the earth signs) |
| Committee #1: | We have to evaluate everything we throw into the trash. Ask: Can this be recycled? |
| Reporter: | They say that 72% of everything being thrown into the trash and landfills today is paper, glass, metal, and plastic that could be recycled. |
| Committee #1: | If we just stepped up recycling efforts, it would help a lot. (have each picketer show a recycle sign as they speak) |
| Picketer 1: | Never, never, never throw away aluminum cans, foil, or pans. |
| Picketer 2: | Stop! Don't throw that glass jar in the trash; recycle it instead. |
| Picketer 3: | There's no excuse! Every piece of paper can be recycled or reused. |

Committee #1:  That's amazing to think that we could get rid of two thirds of our trash and landfill problems if we just recycled.

Committee #2:  What else should we do?

Reporter:  We need to reduce the number of cars or amount of driving we do.

Committee #3:  Drive less?

Committee #1:  We could share rides, make one instead of five trips to the grocery store, plan trips so that we combine several outings into one, push for more efficient cars, walk, ride a bike. The bottom line is DRIVE YOUR CAR LESS.

Reporter:  Plastics are a big problem too. The manufacture and disposal of plastics pollute both the air we breathe and the water we drink.

Committee #1:  Push for less needless packaging and recycle plastic whenever possible.

Reporter:  Then there's foam. And we haven't even talked about disposable diapers and the damage that untreated human waste is causing to our water supply. Or the chemicals lawn companies spray on the grass to create those perfect, golf course looking lawns. That's soil, air, and water pollution all from one source. Those little warning signs that they plant around the edges of the lawn, mean what they say, lawn chemicals kill insects, butterflies, birds, wildlife, and even people.

Committee #1:  Well, it's easy to see that we're not going to solve this problem today.

Reporter:  No, but we can't give up.

Committee #1:  You're right. First, we'll push recycling.

Committee #2:  One of our next big problem areas is with cars, trucks, airplanes, and buses. If we could reduce the number of times we drive each day by half, it would make a huge difference.

Reporter:  You could car pool. Invite a friend to ride with you instead of both of you driving to the same place.

Committee #3:  Plan trips. Don't drive across town for one errand and then an hour later go back for something you forgot to do. Plan ahead.

Committee #2:  Remember that every time you turn the key and start up your car, you are polluting the air you breathe and the water that you drink.

Committee #1:  We're going to need help. Everyone's got to get involved. A small group can't solve the problem that we've all created.

Reporter:  No, but each person who recycles today can rescue about four pounds of trash from the landfill which means less air, water, and soil pollution; so even one person can make a difference.

Committee #1:  We need to mobilize; get some help in here. Come on everybody (clear stage except for Reporter).

Picketers:  Save the Earth. Don't pollute. Start today. Don't delay. Do your part (send people out to pick up all the trash that was thrown over the stage during the play)

Reporter:  You can help too. Pollution can't be solved in one day, but we can save the earth, there's still time, but you, me, everyone, we have to

|               | get started, right this minute. Go home, look at the trash. What have you thrown away that you could have recycled? What about your car? |
|---|---|
| Committee #1: | Combining trips will not only reduce pollution but it will save you money. Join the picket line; stand up for clean air, water, and soil. Give the children of today and tomorrow a cleaner world to live in. |
| Picketers: | (chant) Stomp out pollution. Stomp out pollution. Stomp out pollution. |
| Picketer 1: | Stop! Don't throw that in the trash. Recycle it instead. |
| Picketer 2: | Yuck! This water's brown; and it stinks. |
| Picketer 3: | Give me, clean, clean, clean, clean air to breathe. Give me fresh, fresh, fresh, fresh water to drink (have entire group join in the cheer and wave signs). |
| Reporter: | You can make a difference; so can I; so what are we waiting for? (reporter exits as group picks up on Picketer 3's chant – repeat three times) |

# Chapter 10
# Back to the Classroom

*She is now sixteen years old, a sophomore in high school. Ten months after she began my vowel clustering program, she got her Christmas wish; she was reading at the first grade level. Fourteen months later, she was reading at the second grade level. For nine years, this student failed in reading. The mother was told that her daughter would probably never learn to read. The student was told that she was lazy and not trying, when, in fact she could learn. It was a struggle and continues to be a struggle, but she is reading.*

The example of the young teenager first introduced in Chapter 2 illustrates how the *school-based mental health approach* provides the skill building and counseling needed to help a student erase failure and return to the classroom and work successfully. To take new student-centered methods back to the classroom, first we must get rid of mandated testing; it has been a complete failure and has only increased the failure and inability of teachers to teach and students to learn. We need to teach to the needs of the students, not the needs of a contrived test. In most cases, it is not the students who are failing, or even the teachers, for that matter; instead, it is the methods that we use to teach students in the classroom which have failed and continue to fail every single day. Yes, some students learn; some students will always learn no matter what method you use to teach, but what of the students who are struggling and in many cases failing, not because they cannot learn, but because we are failing to teach them?

Second, we need to drop self-esteem training from public education. The concept of self-esteem has become so distorted that it is doing more harm than good. Feeling good about yourself for receiving all A's on your report card when you cannot even read at the first grade level is neither constructive nor psychologically sound. "Social promotion" and "mandated lowest report card grades" are ridiculous. That is not teaching, and it certainly will not help a student become successful in life. We need to insert self-efficacy training which incorporates positive learning experiences with actual improvement of skills instead of our present distorted use of self-esteem. If a student fails to learn in the classroom, we should then institute a group-centered, after school hands-on program which would reteach the classroom material using a *school-based mental health approach*. A totally hands-on learning-centered approach should be implemented where students could learn at their own pace. Just as the student in our opening example exemplified, all students can learn, if we can only learn how to teach them.

Third, we need to remember that children learn best through their actions, and we need to establish hands-on curriculum and teaching methods for our public school classrooms. We need to train teachers and administrators in hands-on methods. We also need to return to teaching critical thinking and analytical reasoning in the classroom. On a recent mandated state test, over three fourths of the students missed a question asking them to identify which of the three countries was an island: France, the United States, or Haiti. Using a map, most of the students said France. Clearly, students did not understand the meaning of the word "island" nor did they have the reasoning skills to look at a map and figure out the correct answer. We must teach students how to apply and use the information that they are taught. Such is not possible through a panic stricken bombardment of worksheets or mandated testing.

## To Erase Failure in the Classroom

If we want to erase failure in the classroom, we must combine both the academic and psychological needs of the student into every lesson we teach. The *school-based mental health approach* can be used in the classroom as well as in after school or community-based programs. The *school-based mental health approach* combines the academic and psychological needs of the student into every group-centered intervention. The *school-based mental health approach* also stresses prevention. Simply giving a student an F on an assignment or for the semester will not teach or motivate the student to learn the information that he or she needs to know to be successful in life. If a student is failing, then something is wrong; a new approach should be attempted. Perhaps family and community influences are the problem, drugs may be a factor, lack of motivation, or the student simply may not understand and be able to learn through the classroom approach. We must stop simply passing out failing grades or socially passing students on to the next grade. We must stop creating at-risk students. We must pull counseling out of the shadows and put it to work in the classroom, the hallway, and into preventive programs that will stop failure and help students learn and become productive, happy participants in the world in which they live.

There are first grade classrooms where first graders sit and take notes while the teacher lectures. How can we possibly expect a first grader to learn how to read from lecture notes? We cannot entirely blame teachers when they too must comply with the dictates of administrators who select textbooks and dictate teaching strategies. As my university students explained, "we are learning all of these new methods here in your class but we will not be allowed to use any of these methods when we go to teach in the local schools." A quick observation proves their point, 12 worksheets a day in the classroom with video lectures and a packet of 14 worksheets for homework. That is not teaching, and it is no wonder students cannot learn under such cloistered methods.

Change must start at the top and work all the way down to the student. State and federal governments must stop pretending that mandated testing is an effective way to improve classroom instruction. Teaching to a test has never been effective, nor will it ever be. Mandated testing has encouraged some schools to stop teaching spelling because spelling is not covered on the mandated test. Learning to spell is an essential step in becoming educated. Spelling cannot simply be left out or skipped because the mandated test standards do not test spelling.

It's time for a change, a change that benefits students instead of hurting them. Universities must change. Universities must teach evidence-based teaching methods to new prospective teachers and educational research standards must become more rigorous. In some instances, education research has become sloppy, such sloppy research then finds its way into the classroom, with students paying the ultimate price. Educational researchers must raise the standards for educational research. Education is too important to be relegated to second-class practices. There are many university education programs still teaching "whole language" even though such methods were proved unsuccessful over 10 years ago (NRP 2000). New prospective teachers are paying expensive tuition dollars to learn out-of-date, "whole language" teaching methods from fully accredited universities. Accreditation offices simply say "whatever the Dean signs off on is fine with us." Where is the check and balance in such a system? The university students are being cheated and so are the public school children they will later teach.

Universities which train today and tomorrow's teachers and counselors must strive for excellence. The course requirements for becoming a teacher or school counselor should be the most rigorous programs any university offers because teachers and school counselors shape the minds and psychological well-being of tomorrow's society. We can no longer allow tuition-driven education degrees which generate teachers who cannot even write grammatical sentences for student exams, and yes, we do have certified teachers right now in the classroom, who cannot write a sentence that is grammatically correct. How can teachers be expected to teach what they themselves do not know?

## To Erase Failure in School-Based Mental Health

School counseling is in a disastrous state. School counselors have become administrative assistants instead of in-school counselors for students who need help. We simply cannot continue to pretend that the psychological and academic needs of students are not intertwined. We must stop refusing to acknowledge that there is a relationship between learning and well-being. We must open a new door in education and counseling.

As you write the final draft of your prevention program, remember to include counseling, intrinsic motivation, and skill building. It is not enough to simply teach skills, or to conduct therapy, or to motivate. There must be a combination. This combination is what makes group-centered prevention programming successful.

Each program will be different. A program must be designed around the needs of the students in your group, and the *school-based mental health approach* requires that your program meet both the academic and psychological needs of every student in your group. Remember to go back to each chapter and check the trouble-shooting checklists. Also, go back to Chapter 4 and check the needs of your group members. Then ask yourself: Does your program design meet both the academic and psychological needs of your participants?

Remember, even though Step 10 says to write the final draft, you may want to change your design as you test your program through formative evaluations. Even a good program can always be improved.

## *Step 10: Write the Final Draft for Your Group-Centered Prevention Program*

# References

Adelman, H. S., & Taylor, L. (2006). Mental health in schools and public health. *Public Health Report, 121*, 294–298.

Baker, L. M., Dreher, J., & Guthrie, J. T. (Eds.). (2000). *Engaging young readers: Promoting achievement and motivation.* New York: Guilford.

Bandura, A. (1977). Self-efficacy: Toward a unifying theory of behavior change. *Psychological Review, 84*, 191–215.

Bandara, A. (1986). *Social foundations of thought and action: A social cognitive theory.* Englewood Cliffs, NJ: Prentice-Hall.

Bandura, A. (1995). Exercise of personal and collective efficacy in changing societies. In A. Bandura (Ed.), *Self-efficacy in changing societies* (pp. 1–45). New York: Cambridge University Press.

Bandura, A. (1997). *Self-efficacy: The exercise of control.* New York: W. H. Freeman.

Bandura, A., Barbaranelli, C., Vittorio Caprara, G., & Pastorelli, C. (2001). Self-efficacy beliefs as shapers of children's aspirations and career trajectories. *Child Development, 72*, 187–206.

Baumeister, R. F., Campbell, J. D., Krueger, J. I., & Vohs, K. D. (2003). Does high self-esteem cause better performance, interpersonal success, happiness, or healthier lifestyles? *Psychological Science in the Public Interest, 4*, 1–44.

Baumeister, R. F., Campbell, J. D., Krueger, J. I., & Vohs, K. D. (2005). Exploding the self-esteem myth. *Scientific American, 292*, 84–92.

Baumeister, R. F., & Leary, M. (1995). The need to belong: Desire for interpersonal attachments as a fundamental human motivation. *Psychological Bulletin, 117*(3), 497–529.

Berking, M., Orth, U., Wupperman, P., Meier, L. L., & Caspar, F. (2008). Prospective effects of emotion-regulation skills on emotional adjustment. *Journal of Counseling Psychology, 55*, 485–494. doi:10.1037/a0013589.

Brigman, G., & Webb, L. (2007). Student success skills: Impacting achievement through large and small group work. *Group Dynamics: Theory, Research, and Practice, 11*, 283–292. doi:10.1037/1089-2699.11.4.283.

Brooks-Gunn, J. (2003). Do you believe in magic? What we can expect from early childhood intervention programs. *Social Policy Report: Giving Child and Youth Development Knowledge Away, 17*, 3–14.

Brown, S., & Tracy, E. M. (2008). Building communities of practice to advance mental health services in schools. *The Community Psychologist, 41*, 46–49.

Bryant, A., Schulenberg, J., O'Malley, P., Bachman, J., & Johnston, L. (2003). How academic achievement, attitudes, and behaviors relate to the course of substance use during adolescence: A 6-year, multinational longitudinal study. *Journal of Research on Adolescence, 13*, 361–397.

Buhs, E. S., Ladd, G. W., & Herald, S. (2006). Peer exclusion and victimization: Processes that mediate the relation between peer group rejection and children's classroom engagement and achievement? *Journal of Educational Psychology, 98*, 1–13. doi:10.1037/0022-0663.98.1.1.

Catalano, R. F., Mazza, J. J., Harachi, T. W., Abbott, R. D., Haggerty, K. P., & Fleming, C. B. (2003). Raising healthy children through enhancing social development in elementary school: Results after 1.5 years. *Journal of School Psychology, 41*, 143–164.

Clanton Harpine, E. (2005a, August). After-school community-based prevention project. In Carl Paternite (Chair), *Using community science to promote school-based mental health*. Symposium conducted at the annual convention of the American Psychological Association, Washington, DC.

Clanton Harpine, E. (2005b, March). *Play therapy with inner-city children: Interaction of mood and motivation*. Poster presented at the annual convention of the Southwestern Psychological Association, Memphis, TN.

Clanton Harpine, E. (2006, August). *Developing an effective cost-efficient after-school prevention program for community-based organizations*. Paper presented at the annual convention of the American Psychological Association, New Orleans, LA.

Clanton Harpine, E. (2007a, August). *A community-based after-school prevention program: A one year review of the Camp Sharigan program*. Paper presented at the annual convention of the American Psychological Association, San Francisco, CA.

Clanton Harpine, E. (2007b). Applying motivation theory to real-world problems. *Teaching of Psychology, 34*, 111–113.

Clanton Harpine, E. (2007c, July). Therapeutic interventions in schools: After-school group prevention programs. *The Group Psychologist, 17*, 19–20.

Clanton Harpine, E. (2008). *Group interventions in schools: Promoting mental health for at-risk children and youth*. New York: Springer.

Clanton Harpine, E. (2010a). *Erasing failure in the classroom* (Camp Sharigan, a ready-to-use group-centered intervention for grades 1-3 2nd ed., Vol. 1). Aiken, SC: Group-Centered Learning.

Clanton Harpine, E. (2010b). *Erasing failure in the classroom* (Vowel clustering, a ready-to-use classroom style group-centered intervention for teaching irregular vowel sounds to at-risk children and youth, Vol. 2). Aiken, SC: Group-Centered Learning.

Clanton Harpine, E. (2011). Erasing failure in the classroom: Vol. 3. The Reading Orienteering Club, using vowel clustering in an after-school program. Aiken, SC: Group-Centered Learning.

Clanton Harpine, E. (2011). Erasing failure in the classroom: Vol. 5. Sharigan's World Pollution Conference, a Camp Sharigan style week-long ready-to-use group-centered intervention for grades 1-3, Aiken, SC: Group-Centered Learning.

Clanton Harpine, E., & Reid, T. (2009a). Enhancing academic achievement in a Hispanic immigrant community: The role of reading in academic failure and mental health. *School Mental Health, 1*, 159–170. doi:10.1007/s12310-009-9011-z.

Clanton Harpine, E., & Reid, T. (2009b, August). *The community's role in school prevention programs: Today and tomorrow*. Workshop presented at the annual convention of the American Psychological Association, Toronto, Canada.

Cleary, T., & Zimmerman, B. J. (2004). Self-regulation empowerment program: A school-based program to enhance self-regulated and self-motivated cycles of student learning. *Psychology in the Schools, 41*, 537–550.

Condry, J., & Chambers, J. (1978). Intrinsic motivation and the process of learning. In M. R. Lepper & D. Greene (Eds.), *The hidden costs of reward: New perspectives on the psychology of human motivation*. Hillsdale, NJ: Lawrence Erlbaum.

Conyne, R. K. (2004). *Preventive counseling: Helping people to become empowered in systems and settings*. New York: Brunner-Routledge.

Cornelius, M. D., Goldschmidt, L., Day, N. L., & Larkby, C. (2002). Alcohol, tobacco and marijuana use among pregnant teenagers: 6-year follow-up of off-spring growth effects. *Neurotoxicology & Teratology, 24*, 703–710.

Criss, M. M., Pettit, G. S., Bates, J. E., Dodge, K. A., & Lapp, A. L. (2002). Family adversity, positive peer relationships, and children's externalizing behavior: A longitudinal perspective on risk and resilience. *Child Development, 73*, 1220–1237.

Deci, E. L., & Ryan, R. M. (1985). *Intrinsic motivation and self-determination in human behavior*. New York: Plenum.

Deci, E. L., Ryan, R. M., & Williams, G. C. (1995). Need satisfaction and the self-regulation of learning. *Learning and Individual Differences, 8*, 165–183.

Dewey, J. (1997). *Democracy and education: Introduction to the philosophy of education*. Glencoe, IL: Free Press.

Fagan, A. A., Hanson, K., Hawkins, J. D., & Arthur, M. W. (2008). Bridging science to practice: Achieving prevention program implementation fidelity in the community youth development study. *American Journal of Community Psychology, 41*, 235–249. doi:10.1007/s10464-008-9176-x.

Fawson, P. C., & Moore, S. A. (1999). Reading incentive programs: Beliefs and practices. *Reading Psychology, 20*, 325–340.

Flaherty, L. T., & Osher, D. (2003). History of school-based mental health services in the United States. In M. Weist, S. W. Evans, & N. A. Lever (Eds.), *Handbook of school mental health* (pp. 11–22). New York: Kluwer Academic/Plenum Publishers.

Fleming, C. B., Harachi, T. W., Cortes, R. C., Abbott, R. D., & Catalano, R. F. (2004). Level and change in reading scores and attention problems during elementary school as predictors of problem behavior in middle school. *Journal of Emotional and Behavioral Disorders, 12*, 130–144.

Foorman, B. R., Breier, J. I., & Fletcher, J. M. (2003). Interventions aimed at improving reading success: An evidence-based approach. *Developmental Neuropsychology, 24*, 613–639.

Goldschmidt, L., Richardson, G. A., Cornelius, M. D., & Day, N. L. (2004). Prenatal marijuana and alcohol exposure and academic achievement at age 10. *Neurotoxicology & Teratology, 26*, 521–532.

Greenberg, M., Weissberg, R. P., O'Brien, M. U., Zins, J. E., Fredricks, L., Resnick, H., et al. (2003). Enhancing school-based prevention and youth development through coordinated social, emotional, and academic learning. *American Psychologist, 58*, 466–474. doi:10.1037/0003-066X.58.6-7.466.

Herman, K. C., Lambert, S. F., Reinke, W. M., & Ialongo, N. S. (2008). Low academic competence in first grade as a risk factor for depressive cognitions and symptoms in middle school. *Journal of Counseling Psychology, 55*, 400–410. doi:10.1037/a0012654.

Hertz-Lazarowitz, R. (1992). Understanding interactive behaviors: Looking at six mirrors. In R. Hertz-Lazarowitz & N. Miller (Eds.), *Interaction in cooperative groups: The theoretical anatomy of group learning* (pp. 71–101). New York: Cambridge University Press.

Hoag, M. A., & Burlingame, G. M. (1997). Evaluating the effectiveness of child and adolescent group treatment: A meta-analytic review. *Journal of Clinical Child Psychology, 26*, 234–246.

Horne, A. M., Stoddard, J. L., & Bell, C. D. (2007). Group approaches to reducing aggression and bullying in school. *Group Dynamics: Theory, Research, and Practice, 11*, 262–271. doi:10.1037/1089-2699.11.4.262.

Kaplan, A., Lichtinger, E., & Gorodetsky, M. (2009). Achievement goal orientations and self-regulation in writing: An integrative perspective. *Journal of Educational Psychology, 101*, 51–69. doi:10.1037/a0013200.

Kazak, A. E., Hoagwood, K., Weisz, J. R., Hood, K., Kratochwill, T. R., Vargas, L. A., et al. (2010). A meta-systems approach to evidence-based practice for children and adolescents. *American Psychologist, 65*, 85–97. doi:10.1037/a0017784.

Keller, T. A., & Just, M. A. (2009). Altering cortical connectivity: Remediation-induced changes in the white matter of poor readers. *Neuron, 64*, 624–631. doi:10.1016/j.neuron.2009.10.018.

Kratochwill, T. R. (2007). Preparing psychologists for evidence-based school practice: Lessons learned and challenges ahead. *American Psychologist, 62*, 826–843.

Kulic, K. R., Horne, A. M., & Dagley, J. C. (2004). A comprehensive review of prevention groups for children and adolescents. *Group Dynamics: Theory, Research, and Practice, 8*, 139–151. doi:10.1037/1089-2699.8.2.139.

Ladd, G. S., & Dinella, L. M. (2009). Continuity and change in early school engagement: Predictive of children's achievement trajectories from first to eighth grade? *Journal of Educational Psychology, 101*, 190–206. doi:10.1037/a0013153.

Landreth, G. L. (2002). *Play therapy: The art of the relationship*. New York: Brunner-Routledge.

Lepper, M. R., & Greene, D. (1975). Turning play into work: Effects of adult surveillance and extrinsic rewards on children's intrinsic motivation. *Journal of Personality and Social Psychology, 31*, 479–486.

Lewis, B. A., Singer, L. T., Short, E., Minnes, S., Arendt, R., Weishampel, P., et al. (2004). Four-year language outcomes of children exposed to cocaine in utereo. *Neurotoxicology and Teratology, 26*, 617–628.

Lyon, G. R. (1998, April 28). Overview of reading and literacy initiatives. Testimony before the Committee on Labor and Human Resources, Senate Dirkson Building. Retrieved November 27, 2006, from http://www.cdl.org/resourcelibrary/pdf/lyon_testimonies.pdf

Lyon, G. R. (2002). Reading development, reading difficulties, and reading instruction educational and public health issues. *Journal of School Psychology, 40*, 3–6.

Maras, M. A., Macechko, A. L., & Flaspohler, P. D. (2008). Policy possibilities: Exploring the potential of local school wellness policies. *The Community Psychologist, 41*, 49–53.

Maugban, R. R., Loeber, R., & Stouthamer-Loeber, M. (2003). Reading problems and depressed mood. *Journal of Abnormal Child Psychology, 31*, 219–229.

McHugh, R. K., & Barlow, D. H. (2010). The dissemination and implementation of evidence-based psychological treatments: A review of current efforts. *American Psychologist, 65*, 73–84. doi:10.1037/a0018121.

McHugh, R. K., Murray, H. W., & Barlow, D. H. (2009). Balancing fidelity and adaptation in the dissemination of empirically supported treatments: The promise of transdiagnostic interventions. *Behavior Research and Therapy, 47*, 946–953. doi:10.1016/j.brat.2009.07.005.

McWhirter, J. J., McWhirter, B. T., McWhirter, E. H., & McWhirter, R. J. (2007). *At risk youth: A comprehensive response for counselors, teachers, psychologists, and human services professionals* (4th ed.). Belmont, CA: Thomson Brooks/Cole.

Merzenich, M. M. (2001). Cortical plasticity contributing to child development. In J. L. McClelland & R. S. Siegler (Eds.), *Mechanisms of cognitive development: Behavioral and neural perspectives* (pp. 67–95). Mahwah, NJ: Erlbaum.

Meyler, A., Keller, T. A., Cherkassky, V. L., Gabrieli, J. D., & Just, M. A. (2008). Modifying the brain activation of poor readers during sentence comprehension with extended remedial instruction: A longitudinal study of neuroplasticity. *Neuropsychologia, 46*, 2580–2592.

Morris, D., Shaw, B., & Perney, J. (1990). Helping low readers in grades 2 and 3: An after-school volunteer tutoring program. *Elementary School Journal, 91*, 133–150.

Morris, D., Tyner, B., & Perney, J. (2000). Early steps: Replicating the effects of a first-grade reading intervention program. *Journal of Educational Psychology, 92*, 681–693. doi:10.1037//0022-0663.92.4.681.

Nastasi, B. K., Moore, R. B., & Varjas, K. M. (2004). *School-based mental health services: Creating comprehensive and culturally specific programs*. Washington, DC: American Psychological Association.

National Assessment of Educational Progress. (2009). Nation's Report Card: Reading 2009. Retrieved from http://nces.ed.gov/nations report card/pdf/main2009/2010458.pdf

National Reading Panel, (2000). *Teaching children to read: An evidence-based assessment of the scientific research literature on reading and its implications for reading instruction* (NIH Publication No. 00-4754). Washington, DC: National Institute for Literacy.

Nelson, C. A., & Bosquet, M. (2000). Neurobiology of fetal and infant development: Implications for infant mental health. In C. H. Zeanah Jr. (Ed.), *Handbook of infant mental health* (2nd ed.). New York: Guilford Press.

Nelson, G., Westhues, A., & MacLeod, J. (2003). A meta-analysis of longitudinal research on preschool prevention programs for children. *Prevention and Treatment, 6*, Article 0031a. Retrieved May 9, 2005, from http://journals.apa.org/prevention/volume 6/preoo60031a.html

O'Brien Caughy, M., Murray Nettles, S., & O' Campo, P. J. (2008). The effect of residential neighborhood on child behavior problems in first grade. *American Journal of Community Psychology, 42*, 39–50.

Obiakor, F. E. (2001). *It even happens in "good" schools: Responding to cultural diversity in today's classrooms*. Thousand Oaks, CA: Sage.

Pintrich, P. R., & Schunk, D. H. (2002). *Motivation in education: Theory, research, and applications* (2nd ed.). NJ: Prentice Hall.

Posthuma, B. W. (2002). *Small groups in counseling and therapy: Process and leadership* (4th ed.). Boston, MA: Allyn and Bacon.

Rayner, K., Foorman, B. R., Perfetti, C. A., Pesetsky, D., & Seidenberg, M. S. (2001). How psychological science informs the teaching of reading. *Psychological Science in the Public Interest, 2*, 31–74. doi:10.1111/1529-10006.00004.

Reeve, J., Nix, G., & Hamm, D. (2003). The experience of self-determination in intrinsic motivation and the conundrum of choice. *Journal of Educational Psychology, 95*, 347–392.

Richardson, G. A., Goldschmidt, L., & Willford, J. (2008). The effects of prenatal cocaine use on infant development. *Neurotoxicology and Teratology, 30*, 96–106.

Royse, D., Thyer, B. A., Padgett, D. K., & Logan, T. K. (2006). *Program evaluation: An introduction* (4th ed.). Belmont, CA: Thomson Brooks/Cole.

Rudolph, K. D., Kurlakowsky, K. D., & Conley, C. S. (2001). Developmental and social-contextual origins of depressive control-related beliefs and behavior. *Cognitive Therapy and Research, 25*, 447–475.

Ryan, R. M., & Deci, E. L. (2000). Intrinsic and extrinsic motivations: Classic definitions and new directions. *Contemporary Educational Psychology, 25*, 54–67.

Salovey, P., Rothman, A. J., Detweiler, J. B., & Steward, W. T. (2000). Emotional states physical health. *American Psychologist, 55*, 110–121.

Satcher, D. (2000). Children's mental health: A report of the Surgeon General – Executive summary. *Professional Psychology: Research and Practice, 31*, 5–13.

Seligman, M. E. P. (1990). *Learned optimism.* New York: Simon & Schuster.

Seligman, M. E. P. (2007). *The optimistic child: A proven program to safeguard children against depression and build lifelong resilience.* New York: Houghton Mifflin.

Seligman, M. E. P., & Csikzentmihalyi, M. (2000). Positive psychology: An introduction. *American Psychologist, 55*, 5–14.

Schunk, D. H., & Pajares, F. (2005). Competence perceptions and academic functioning. In A. J. Elliot & C. S. Dweck (Eds.), *Handbook of competence and motivation* (pp. 85–104). New York: The Guilford Press.

Stenhouse, L. (1975). *An introduction to curriculum research and development.* London: Heinemann.

Sternberg, R. J. (2005). Intelligence, competence, and expertise. In A. J. Elliot & C. S. Dweck (Eds.), *Handbook of competence and motivation* (pp. 15–30). New York: The Guilford Press.

Sternberg, R. J., & Grigorenko, E. L. (Eds.). (2002). *The general factor of intelligence: How general is it?* Mahwah, NJ: Lawrence Erlbaum.

Sternberg, R. J., Wagner, R. K., Williams, W. M., & Horvath, J. A. (1997). Testing common sense. In D. Russ-Eft, H. Preskill, & C. Sleezer (Eds.), *Human resource development review: Research and implications* (pp. 102–132). Thousand Oaks, CA: Sage.

Sussman, S., Earleywine, M., Wills, T., Cody, C., Biglan, T., Dent, C., et al. (2004). The motivation, skills, and decision-making model of "drug abuse" prevention. *Substance Use and Misuse, 39*, 1971–2016.

Swann, W. B., Jr., Chang-Schneider, C., & Larsen McClarty, K. (2007). Do people's self-views matter? Self-concept and self-esteem in everyday life. *American Psychologist, 62*, 84–94.

Taba, H. (1962). *Curriculum development: Theory and practice*. New York: Harcourt, Brace and World.

Taylor, S. E., Kemeny, M. E., Reed, G. M., Bower, J. E., & Gruenewald, T. L. (2000). Psychological resources, positive illustions, and health. *American Psychologist, 55*, 99–109.

Thompson, M. C. (2000). *Word within the word* (2nd ed., Vol. 1). New York: Royal Fireworks Press.

Thorkildsen, T. A. (2002). Literacy as a lifestyle: Negotiating the curriculum to facilitate motivation. *Reading and Writing Quarterly, 18*, 321–328.

U. S. Public Health Service. (2000). Report of the Surgeon General's Conference on Children's Mental Health: A national action agenda. Washington, DC: U.S. Department of health and Human Services. Retrieved from http://www.gurgeongeneral.gov/library/mentalhealth/chapter3/sec.1.html

Urdan, T., & Turner, J. C. (2005). Competence motivation in the classroom. In A. J. Elliot & C. S. Dweck (Eds.), *Handbook of competence and motivation* (pp. 297–317). New York: The Guilford Press.

Vallerand, R. J., Fortier, M. S., & Guay, F. (1997). Self-determination and persistence in a real-life setting: Toward a motivational model of high school dropout. *Journal of Personality and Social Psychology, 72*, 1161–1176.

Wandersman, A., Duffy, J., Flaspohler, P., Norman, R., Lubell, K., Stillman, L., et al. (2008). Bridging the gap between prevention research and practice: The interactive systems framework for dissemination and implementation. *American Journal of Community Psychology, 41*, 171–181. doi:10.1007/s10464-008-9174-z.

Wandersman, A., & Florin, P. (2003). Community interventions and effective prevention. *American Psychologist, 58*, 441–448. doi:10.1037/0003-066X.58.6-7.441.

Webb, N. M. (1992). Testing a theoretical model of student interaction and learning in small groups. In R. Hertz-Lazarowitz & N. Miller (Eds.), *Interaction in cooperative groups: The theoretical anatomy of group learning* (pp. 102–119). New York: Cambridge University Press.

Weinstein, R. S. (2006). Reaching higher in community psychology: Social problems, social settings, and social change. *American Journal of Community Psychology, 37*, 9–20. doi:10.1007/s10464-005-9008-1.

Weissberg, R., Kumpfer, K., & Seligman, M. (2003). Prevention that works for children and youth: An introduction. *American Psychologist, 58*, 425–432. doi:10.1037/0003-066X.58.6-7.425.

Weist, M. D. (1997). Expanded school mental health services: A national movement in progress. In T. H. Ollendick & R. J. Prinz (Eds.), *Advances in clinical child psychology* (Vol. 19, pp. 319–352). New York: Plenum Press.

Weist, M. D., & Paternite, C. E. (2006). Building an interconnected policy-training-practice-research agenda to advance school mental health. *Education and Treatment of Children, 29*, 173–196.

Weisz, J. R., Jensen, A. L., & McLeod, B. D. (2004). Development and dissemination of child and adolescent therapies: Milestones, methods, and a new deployment-focused model. In E. Hersen & P. S. Jensen (Eds.), *Psychosocial treatments for child and adolescent disorders: Empirically-based approaches* (2nd ed.). Washington, DC: American Psychological Association.

Wills, T. A., Yaeger, A. M., & Sandy, J. M. (2003). Buffering effect of religiosity for adolescent substance use. *Psychology of Addictive Behaviors, 17*, 24–31.

Yalom, I. D., & Leszcz, M. (2005). *The theory and practice of group psychotherapy* (5th ed.). New York: Basic Books.

Zimmerman, B. J., Kitsantas, A., Elliot, A. J., & Dweck, C. S. (2005). The hidden dimension of personal competence: Self-regulated learning and practice. In *Handbook of competence and motivation* (pp. 509–526). New York: The Guilford Press.

# Index

## A

Academic and psychological needs, 1, 6, 24, 30, 37, 142, 144
Academic failure, 3, 4, 8, 23, 66, 99, 123
Academic success, 7, 66, 68, 70
ADHD. *See* Attention deficit hyperactivity disorder
After-school programs, 1, 9–11, 27, 28, 53, 56, 68–70, 79, 82, 99, 101, 102, 117, 122, 123
At-risk children, 1–21, 27, 28, 30, 31, 53, 57, 61, 74, 102, 104
Attention deficit hyperactivity disorder (ADHD), 40–42, 50, 65, 70, 79, 99, 101, 122, 124, 130

## B

Behavior problems, 8, 40, 50, 53, 65, 117, 118
Blue ribbon schools program, 6
Brain, 5, 19, 67

## C

*Camp Sharigan*, 1, 2, 13, 15, 27, 28, 30, 37, 40, 47, 55, 56, 59–61, 65, 68, 69, 71, 73–77, 79, 81–85, 87–89, 99, 101, 102, 104, 105, 107, 118, 120–122, 125, 129, 130
Change, 5–8, 10–18, 20, 21, 25–32, 42, 43, 47–63, 66, 67, 69, 74–77, 80, 83–85, 107, 108, 118–120, 122–125, 128, 137, 138, 143, 144
Children, 1–21, 23, 26–28, 30, 31, 34, 35, 38, 40, 41, 43, 47–50, 52–63, 65, 66, 68–71, 73–78, 81–84, 87–91, 93, 96, 99–102, 104–109, 112–115, 118, 120–124, 126, 129–131, 133, 140, 142, 143

Classroom, 1–4, 6, 7, 10, 11, 13, 15, 23, 25–28, 30, 31, 34, 35, 38, 40, 42–44, 47–57, 60, 65–70, 79, 80, 82, 84, 87, 88, 90, 93, 100, 101, 103–108, 117–127, 129, 130, 141–144
Classroom reading circles, 54
Classroom teacher, 38, 40, 142, 143
Community programs, 9
Community's involvement, 9
Constructive interactive situations, 85
Counseling needs of students, 2
Counselors, 3, 7–9, 12, 13, 42, 44, 65, 82, 122, 143

## D

Depressive symptoms, 13, 66
Design example, 15, 30–31, 40–43, 59–61, 73–76, 87–89, 104–106, 129–130

## E

Effective group interaction, 81
Evidence-based programs, 10–14, 107
Expectations, 59, 67, 68, 72, 74, 75, 81
Extrinsic motivators, 65, 66, 69, 76, 83
Extrinsic rewards, 15, 63, 65, 67, 100

## F

Formative evaluation, 52–57, 59–61, 144

## G

Good intentions, 9, 11, 12
Group, 1–4, 6–16, 23–97, 100–109, 117–144
Group atmosphere, 50, 106

CPSIA information can be obtained at www.ICGtesting.com
225415LV00003B/10/P

9 781441 972477